TWAYNE'S WORLD AUTHORS SERIES
A Survey of the World's Literature

SPAIN

Janet W. Diaz, Texas Tech University

EDITOR

Concha Espina

TWAS 559

Concha Espina

CONCHA ESPINA

By MARY LEE BRETZ

Rutgers University

TWAYNE PUBLISHERS

A DIVISION OF G. K. HALL & CO., BOSTON

Library of Congress Cataloging in Publication Data

Bretz, Mary Lee.
Concha Espina.

(Twayne's world author series ; TWAS 559 : Spain)
Bibliography: p. 152-53
Includes index.
1. Espina, Concha, 1869-1955—Criticism and interpretation.
PQ6609.S5Z554   863'.6'2   79-9787
ISBN 0-8057-6401-1

Contents

About the Author

Mary Lee Bretz holds an A.B. from Trinity College (Washington, D.C.), and M.A. from Stanford University and Ph.D. from the University of Maryland. She is presently an Assistant Professor of Spanish and Portuguese at Rutgers College of Rutgers University. She has published on nineteenth and twentieth century Spanish literature in various journals including *Cuadernos Hispanoamericanos, Papeles de Son Armadans, The American Hispanist,* and *Boletín de la Biblioteca de Menéndez Pelayo.* She is also the author of the book *La evolución novelística de Pío Baroja.*

Preface

After having been twice nominated for the Nobel Prize for Literature and once losing the prestigious award by a single vote, Concha Espina's fame has declined in recent years. With the exception of several articles and a biography written by her daughter, the centennial anniversary of her birth—celebrated in 1969—provoked little interest. The reasons for this critical silence are multiple. Concha Espina belonged to no literary group and left no literary successors. Whereas writers of equal or lesser merit demand attention from a purely historical point of view, her work is of marginal importance in terms of the development and transmission of literary trends. In addition, the years following an author's death are normally characterized by a loss of recognition as new modes of expression displace the old. From today's perspective, much of Concha Espina's work seems decidedly outmoded and it is difficult to judge whether future readers will respond similarly.

Another cause of Concha Espina's decline in fame is strictly political. During the last fifty years, Spanish critics outside of Spain and to a large degree within its national frontiers have shown considerably less interest in writers of conservative leaning than in those identified with the left. Although Concha Espina does not always identify with rightist politics, she is popularly perceived as a Falangist supporter and this does not enhance her desirability as a literary subject.

In part, the critical silence of recent years is justified. Concha Espina is a writer of extremely uneven merit whose weakest works hardly warrant attention. On the other hand, she published a number of excellent novels that should definitely not be overlooked by the student of Spanish literature. In particular, the novel on the people of Maragatería represents a unique contribution to Spanish Regionalist literature and it alone justifies Concha Espina's inclusion among the outstanding Spanish writers of the past century. Aside from the literary value of her work, Concha Espina's writing is of interest as a sociological document. More than most authors, she serves as a barometer for the socio-political attitudes of the moderate to conservative middle class of her period. If the literary repercussions of twentieth-century Spanish history are to be fully understood, Concha Espina and those of her persuasion must be given more attention than they have received in the past.

Furthermore, the fact that Concha Espina is decidedly not a member of the intellectual community increases her value as a spokesperson for a numerically large and politically influential group. Baroja, Unamuno, Pérez de Ayala, and the members of the Generation of 1927 are unquestionably more important from a strictly artistic point of view, but they are in many respects less in tune with the values of Spain's middle class. Concha Espina's view of the causes and consequences of the Civil War, her changing social attitudes over the course of her production, and her interpretation of Hispanic character provide a valuable measure of national sentiment which makes the events of 1900-1950 more comprehensible to those seeking a feeling for Spain's history.

A final justification for continued interest in Concha Espina's work lies in the fact that she is a woman writing at a time when very few Spanish women entered the literary field and none succeeded, as she did, in supporting themselves solely on the basis of their publications. The fact that Concha Espina is a woman cannot be ignored in a critical analysis of her work. It explains her lack of contact with contemporary writers during the crucial formative period, her susceptibility to the opinions of her critics, and a number of other characteristics that I will examine in my study.

In view of the multifaceted quality of her writing and the various points of interest which I propose to discuss, I have followed no single method in the analysis of Concha Espina's production, preferring to vary my approach according to the character of each work. In all cases, I have included some discussion of the artistic element but on a number of occasions, historical or sociological considerations are given priority. With the exception of a few of Concha Espina's privately published poems and her early newspaper articles, this study covers all of her publications, a good number of which are not included in her *Complete Works*.

Since her production is often inextricably tied to historical developments and because her works do not fall into easily definable groupings, I have organized the study according to the order of publication. The chapter divisions correspond only roughly to various periods in her career, as Concha Espina's evolution follows an irregular pattern. From 1904 to 1953 she published close to fifty volumes. Among these, only a small number of the early works and her Civil War literature fit into thematic or ideological groupings. The fact that she never truly establishes a definitive rhythm is characteristic of her production and reflects a failure to identify and maintain an artistic form compatible with her literary aims or talents. This failure inhibits the cultivation of a definitive literary personality and ultimately diminishes the value of her work. As I shall attempt to illustrate in the following pages, Concha Espina achieves a great deal in the course of her career but she is unable to sustain the force that gives rise to her best achievements.

MARY LEE BRETZ

Rutgers University

Chronology

1869 Concha Espina born in Santander, Spain.[1]

1891 Mother dies.

1892 Marries Ramón de la Serna and leaves for Valparaíso, Chile with her husband. Son Ramón born in Valparaíso.

1895– Son Víctor born in Valparaíso. Returns to Spain with husband
1896 and children.

1898– Son José born in Mazcuerras, Spain.
1899

1900– Daughter Josefina born in Mazcuerras, Spain.
1901

1903– Son José dies.
1904

1904 Publishes *Mis flores* [My flowers].

1907 Son Luis born. Wins regional literary prize for *"La riada"* ["The rapids"].

1908 Separates from her husband and moves to Madrid.

1909 Publishes *La niña de Luzmela* [The girl from Luzmela].

1910 *La ronda de los galanes* [The lover's patrol] and *Despertar para morir* [To wake up and die].

1911 *Agua de nieve* [The woman and the sea].

1914 *La esfinge maragata* [Mariflor], winner of the Royal Academy's Fastenrath Prize.

1916 *Mujeres del Quijote* [Women of the Quijote] and *La rosa de los vientos* [The rose of the winds].

1917 Publishes *Don Quijote en Barcelona* [Don Quijote in Barcelona], a lecture originally given in Barcelona, and *Ruecas de marfil* [Ivory distaffs].

1918 *Naves en el mar* [Boats in the sea] and *Talín* [Wild canary].

1919 *El príncipe del cantar* [The prince of song] and *El jayón* [The foundling], winner of the Espinosa Cortina Prize.

1920 *El metal de los muertos* [The metal of the dead] and *Pastorelas* [Rustic melodies].

1921 *Dulce Nombre* [The red beacon].

1922 *Simientes* [Seeds] and *Cuentos* [Stories]. Joins son Ramón in Germany and travels through the country.
1923 *El caliz rojo* [The red chalice].
1924 *Tierras del Alquilón* [Lands of the north wind], winner of the Castillo de Chirel Prize.
1925 *El secreto de un disfraz* [The secret of a disguise].
1926 *Altar mayor* [High altar], winner of the National Prize for Literature.
1927 *Las niñas desaparecidas* [The girls who disappeared]. Statue and garden in her honor dedicated in Santander, Spain.
1928 *El goce de robar* [The joy of robbery]. Represents Alfonso XIII on cultural mission to Cuba, Santo Domingo, and Puerto Rico. Attends Middlebury College as Visiting Professor.
1929 *La virgen prudente* [The prudent virgin].
1930 *Siete rayos del sol* [Seven sun rays] and *Copa de horizontes* [A cupfull of horizons].
1931 *Llama de cera* [Wax flame].
1932 *Singladuras* [Day's run].
1933 *Entre la noche y el mar* [Between the night and the sea] and *Candelabro* [Candelabra].
1934 *Flor de ayer* [Yesterday's flower].
1935 Serves as Cultural Ambassador to the Fourth Centennial Celebration of the Founding of Lima.
1936 Outbreak of Civil War. House Arrest in Luzmela, Spain.
1937 *Retaguardia* published in Nationalist held Burgos.
1938 *Luna roja* [Red moon]; *Esclavitud y libertad—Diario de una prisionera* [Slavery and liberty — diary of a prisoner]; *Alas invencibles* [Invincible wings].
1939 *Princesas del martirio* [Martyred princesses]. Loses eyesight.
1940 *Casilda de Toldedo* [Casilda of Toledo]. Writes the unpublished play *La tiniebla encendida* [Enlightened darkness].
1942 *La otra* [The other one]; *Moneda blanca* [White coin]; *Fraile menor* [The lesser friar].
1943 *La segunda mies* [The second crop].
1944 *Victoria en América* [Victoria in America].
1947 *El más fuerte* [The strongest one].
1950 *Un valle en el mar* [A valley in the sea].
1951 *De Antonio Machado a su grande y secreto amor* [From Antonio Machado to his great and secret love].
1953 *Una novela de amor* [A novel of love].
1955 Concha Espina dies in Madrid, Spain.

CHAPTER 1

From Provincial Roots to World Fame

I *The Early Years*

CONCHA Espina, baptized Concepción Jesusa Basilisa Tagle y Espina, was the seventh of ten children born to Ascensión Tagle de Espina and Víctor Espina. Doña Ascensión, the daughter of *hidalgos* (rural gentry), owned property in Santillana del Mar and Mazcuerras, two small villages in the Cantabrian Mountains of the northern Spanish Province of Santander.[1] Concha Espina's father was originally from Oviedo, in the Asturian region, but relocated in the coastal city of Santander after his marriage. Like his wife, he came from a landowning family and the young couple lived comfortably on their inheritance, spending winters in Santander and summers at the family manor in Mazcuerras.

It was in the busy port of Santander that Concha Espina was born in 1869. Her childhood was in all respects typical of the period: she attended a convent school and she was instructed at home by private tutors in piano, embroidery, dance and culture. As the novelist herself recalled in 1928, she was taught to appreciate and enjoy the advantages of a bourgeois society but was not prepared to face adversity. It was assumed that she would never have need of those skills necessary for economic self-sufficiency. Although she showed an early interest in poetry, there was little in her background or environment to encourage her literary talents. With the exception of a few religious books, her parents possessed no library. Furthermore, there was little precedent in Spain for women writers. Rosalía de Castro, the Galician poet, published her first volume of poetry in 1863 in Galician but her poems in Spanish were not published until 1884. Among those women who did most to further the cause of women writers, Emilia Pardo Bazán did not become a national figure until after 1883. Although her example was most assuredly an inspiration for Concha Espina in her later years, in the initial stages of her literary development, there were no models for her to follow.

Somewhat embarassed by her poetic endeavors, Concha Espina found her only encouragement in her mother, who persuaded the twelve-year-old poet to publish some of her work in a local newspaper. For the present, other aspects of Concha Espina's development took precedence over her literary interests, as is clearly shown in her letters to a childhood friend. Written between 1888 and 1891, the letters are devoted primarily to a description of Concha Espina's newest dresses, her social life, religious events, and the marriages and engagements of her friends.[2] In all respects, her interests are typical of a teenage girl in the late nineteenth century.

Religion played an important role in the Espina home where doña Ascensión devoted a great deal of her time to works of charity and visits to the homes of the sick. From her parents, Concha Espina inherited a strongly religious spirit and a sense of obligation toward the needy and oppressed. Although later experiences were to modify many of her early values, in essence they remained the same throughout her life. Much of her work is an attempt to reaffirm traditional values in the context of modern society. From her childhood she also retained a deep appreciation for the Cantabrian region and its traditions. Although Concha Espina's novels transcend the limitations of Regionalism, some of her best pages bring alive the people and the spirit of her native province. In this as in other aspects, her initial experiences carry over into her adult life and into her literary production. Like many novelists, she recreates time and time again the setting and atmosphere of her early years even while being led further and further from the world of her childhood.

II *Death, Marriage, and Poverty*

When Concha Espina was twenty-one and twenty-two, a series of events occurred that radically changed the direction of her life.[3] After caring for a sick woman, her mother contracted infectious pneumonia and died. The family grief was compounded by Víctor Espina's financial losses and subsequent bankruptcy. The expense of raising and educating seven children could not be met by the income from the family properties. To supplement his earnings, Víctor had established a shipping firm in partnership with Concha Espina's godfather. Víctor — a handsome, worldly man, with a taste for the better things in life—unfortunately was not much of a businessman. He preferred the pleasures of a horse ride or a card game in the local men's club to paperwork in the firm's office. Initially the business prospered, but even before the death of his wife, the shipping firm was in financial trouble. For two years, the family managed to live off its inheritance but after doña Ascensión died, her husband was forced to sell his lands to pay his debts.

Shortly after her mother's death, Concha Espina met and became engaged to Ramón de la Serna, the son of a wealthy family with financial interests in Chile. At that time, Ramón was planning to go to Valparaíso to administer his family's fortune, then in the hands of administrators and rapidly disappearing through poor management. Concha Espina was forced to choose between a long separation and a hurried marriage. She decided to marry Ramón and the couple set out for Chile soon after the wedding. Although at twenty-two she was not the child bride that many critics and biographers have described, her circumstances did not enable her to clearly weigh the implications of her decision. Deprived of emotional and financial security by the recent loss of her mother and her family's economic situation, she was disoriented and lonely. In this state, Ramón's decisiveness and energy must have appeared all the more attractive. Concha Espina did not, however, enter her marriage without misgivings. According to her daughter Josefina, the night before her wedding she confided her doubts in a letter to a family friend and expressed concern that she had not given enough thought to the matter. Whatever the reason for her fears, the next sixteen years proved that they were not unfounded.

III   *The Years in Chile and the Beginnings of a Career*

The young couple spent three years in Chile, where Ramón attempted unsuccessfully to defend his family's interests. Of their five children, Ramón and Víctor were born in Chile. With little income to support them, Concha Espina took her first steps toward independence. According to her own testimony, while leaving church one night she was given a copy of *El Porteño*, a local newspaper sponsored by the head of the diocese. [4] The following day, Concha Espina visited the editor-priest with some of her poetry in the hope that he would include it in *El Porteño*. Her work was accepted and she was paid generously for it, probably more out of sympathy for her situation than in keeping with editorial policy. Nevertheless, her first success gave her the confidence to submit articles to other newspapers and she was soon a paid correspondent for *El Correo Español* of Buenos Aires.

Temperamental differences had already created marital tension, and Concha Espina's journalism contributed further to the conflict. Her daughter describes Ramón as a domineering husband with a violent temper who resented his wife's growing independence.[5] At this time, Concha Espina rejected the idea of separation and attempted to reconcile her role as wife, mother, and writer. While the years in Chile represent a critical period in her life, experiences there are invariably recalled with pleasure by the novelist. Chile and its society opened her eyes to the rich diversity of Hispanic cultures and her exposure to new forms of life undoubtedly helped to broaden her vision.[6] When she and Ramón returned to Spain, she brought with her not only personal disillusionment but a counterbalancing confidence in her artistic abilities and a knowledge of life that enabled her to pursue her career.

IV   *The Termination of a Marriage and the First Novels*

After their return to Spain, Concha and Ramón set up residence in Mazcuerras, later renamed Luzmela in honor of the novelist. Her first novel takes place in Mazcuerras, which she calls Luzmela in the book. The couple spent the next five years in the small town and two more children were born to them there: José, who died at the age of five, and Josefina, who was later to write her mother's biography. In Luzmela, Concha Espina resumed her contact with the Menéndez y Pelayo family. It was Enrique who encouraged Concha Espina to leave the isolation of Luzmela. Subsequently the family moved in with Ramón's mother and her children in Cabezón de la Sal. It was also Enrique who wrote the prologue to *Mis flores* [My flowers], Concha Espina's first book which was published in 1904. For the moment, Concha Espina continued to write poetry but, following the suggestion of Marcelino Menéndez Pelayo she turned to the narrative genres.

It was probably Concha Espina's desire for a place of her own in which she could write without interruption that caused her to leave her in-laws' and move to a smaller house in the village. There, Luis, her last child. was born. Concha Espina continued to lead a secluded life, partly due to her unhappy marriage and partly because she wanted to devote herself to her writing. During this period she continued to contribute to *El Correo Español* of Buenos Aires as well as to a number of Spanish newspapers, generally hiding her identity behind various masculine pennames. At about this time her short story *"La riada"* ["The rapids"] won first prize in a local literary competition and she began work on her first novel, *La niña de Luzmela* [The girl from Luzmela]. Simultaneously, she wrote a number of short stories later published in *Pastorelas* [Rural melodies].

As Concha Espina's reputation and dedication to her work increased, her marital situation deteriorated. On one occasion Ramón ripped up some of her writings and left them in pieces on the floor of her study. The incident confirmed her decision to separate and with the support of her own as well as her husband's family, she arranged for an excellent job offer for Ramón in Mexico, probably hoping to minimize the effects of the separation. With Ramón's departure, Concha Espina was free to pursue her literary career. In 1908, this implied relocating in Madrid, the center of Spain's publishing industry, and the only place where a woman could hope to be successful in the field of literature.

It should be remembered that Concha Espina began to write when women authors were very much an anomaly in Spain. Although Rosalía de Castro and Emilia Pardo Bazán had already broken many of the barriers, neither had attempted to earn a livelihood from writing. Rosalía was married to a respected historian and even though their economic situation was quite modest, economic factors were minimal in her decision to publish her poetry. In the case of Pardo Bazán, her personal fortune was considerable and she had no need to turn to literature as a means of support. For Concha Espina, literature was to be her sole source of income and in this sense, she was a "first" in the history of Spanish women writers. Her economic situation had not improved since her return from Chile and the move to Madrid itself was beyond her means. Only by selling an emerald and diamond ring was she able to afford the trip. With enough money to get her started, she set out for Madrid with the three younger children, having sent her oldest son to London to pursue his studies.

V   The First Years in Madrid and the Struggle for Literary Fame

Concha Espina soon discovered the difficulties that were to confront her as a single woman in Spanish society. She succeeded in finding a suitable apartment, with the prescribed view of the mountains, but was told that without her husband's authorization she could not legally sign a contract, not even when the contract

pertained to the sale and publication of her own work. The immediate
problem of renting the apartment was solved by Julia de los Ríos, the
servant who accompanied Concha Espina to Madrid and was to
manage the domestic affairs of the household for years to come.
Having recently had some shoes repaired by a cobbler who set up
shop in a neighborhood doorway, Julia asked the itinerant craftsman
to sign the papers for her mistress. Later, Ramón gave his full
authorization so that his wife could negotiate freely with her
publishers.

In Madrid, Concha Espina continued her solitary life style,
dividing her activities between family and work with little time or
interest for anything else. In 1909, *The Girl from Luzmela* appeared
and the sales were favorable. *Despertar para morir* [To wake up and
die] and *Agua de nieve* [translated to English as The woman and the
sea] followed in 1910 and 1911. Her reputation was now sufficiently
established to attract the attention of publishers, one of whom
attempted to steer her in the direction of the more lucrative erotic
novel. In addition to the moral question, the suggestion ran counter
to the novelist's personal view of art. Classifying herself as a writer of
"*la alta novela*" ("the high novel"), Concha Espina conceived her
work as the transmission of Christian values and steadfastly refused to
accomodate the purely commercial aspects of literature.

In her weakest novels, character and plot development are lost in a
poetic and sometimes exaggerated exaltation of moral or spiritual
ideals. Although the same ideals prevail in the best of her works, in
these the ambiguities of human existence are not sacrificed to a
personal value system. Such is the case with *La esfinge maragata*
[Mariflor], a magnificent portrait of life in the remote and culturally
singular district of León. Based on her observations of Maragatería,
where she spent several months in her sister's home, the novel
earned her literary fame and the prestigious Fastenrath Prize,
awarded by the Spanish Royal Academy.

VI *The Reaction of the Literary Community*

Concha Espina's successes continued without interruption in the
following years. She was honored by Alfonso XIII with the Ribbon of
the Ladies of María Christina, her portrait was painted for the New
York-based Hispanic Society of America and two of her works of this
period won literary awards: the Espinosa Cortina Prize for her play *El
jayón* [The foundling] and the National Prize for Literature for her

novel *Altar mayor* [High altar]. Nonetheless, her success was not applauded in all quarters. Articles of protest followed the award of the National Prize for Literature. Her son Víctor writes with disgust of the literary "establishment" that remained hostile and resentful of her triumphs.[7] Concha Espina herself writes humorously of the famous novelist and critic, Azorín, and his contempt for women writers. Shortly after her arrival in Madrid, a friend suggested that she give him an autographed copy of *The Girl from Luzmela* which he would personally deliver to Azorín, then a critic for the newspaper *ABC*. Several days later Concha Espina found the same copy, complete with her dedication, in a used book store.[8]

Others in the literary "establishment" were considerably more receptive, as the novelist repeatedly recognized. With time her defenders and friends grew to include the playwright Eduardo Marquina, the sociologist and doctor Angel Pulido, the novelist Ricardo León, the poets Gerardo Diego and Federico García Lorca as well as Santiago Ramón y Cajal, the famous histologist and Nobel Prize winner. The visitors to Concha Espina's house in Madrid became so numerous that her work was constantly interrupted until she decided to set a fixed time when she would receive her friends.

During this period, the family spent summers in Comillas, making frequent visits to Concha Espina's father, now permanently retired in Luzmela. Concha Espina's passion for the small town of her ancestors continued until her death and she subsequently abandoned Comillas for Luzmela. As noted earlier, traditions were of great importance to Concha Espina. She was not, however, indifferent to the latest discoveries, whether literary or scientific. In 1916, aviation was in its infancy in Spain and the novelist eagerly accepted an invitation to fly with Juan Pombo, a childhood friend and aviator. When she confided her plans to Enrique Menédez Pelayo and his wife, they were violently opposed, warning that Pombo's landing gear had broken down and was tied together with ropes. Notwithstanding their misgivings, Concha Espina boarded the plane and landed without incident. In her short story *"Talín"* ["Wild canary"], she recreated the wonders of flight in an age when it had not yet become a common experience.

The same spirit of adventure enabled her to research her novel of the miners' life in Río Tinto. It was probably her father's work as administrator of the Ujo mines that sparked her interest in the matter. After visiting a number of mines in Northern Spain, she spent time in the Andalucian town of Nerva. There the only available lodgings were in a run-down tavern where traveling bands of entertainers normally stayed. As the owner of the house casually informed her, the night before a Chinese acrobat had died in the bed where Concha Espina was to sleep. From Nerva, the novelist made numerous excursions to the local mines, going underground more than once to familiarize herself with the miner's working conditions. Based on Concha Espina's personal observations, *The Metal of the Dead* is a powerful portrait of life in the mines. It earned her a nomination for the Nobel Prize for Literature.

VII *International Fame and the Years of Travel*

Concha Espina always expressed a great love of travel. Family responsibilities and financial problems had prevented her indulging this passion in previous years. In the early 1920's a series of events caused her to leave Spain for the first time since her return from Chile. At this time, her oldest son Ramón was studying Philosophy and Letters at the University of Madrid, where the noted critic and philologist Julio Cejador y Frauca was a professor of Latin. Apparently Cejador made life miserable for the few women enrolled in his classes. After one incident, Ramón publicly protested and stormed out of the room. With a powerful enemy in the Madrid faculty, he decided to pursue his studies in Germany. World War I had recently ended and when the novelist did not hear from her son, she decided to go to Germany with her two youngest children. The family joined Ramón in Berlin. Ramón was not in good health and under doctor's orders to rest, he and his mother left for the peaceful North Sea Island of Helgoland.

The German landscape and life in postwar Germany appear in a number of Concha Espina's stories and serve as the background for her novel *El caliz rojo* [The red chalice]. Exposure to a nonHispanic society confirmed Concha Espina's faith in the values and traditions of her homeland, and the exaltation of Spain's heritage that appears in *The Red Chalice* recurs time and time again during the next years. Germany also awakened her interest in the Jewish people, particularly the Sephardim, the Jews of Spanish origin. One of the main characters in *The Red Chalice* is a portrait of the displaced Sephardic Jew who longs for a permanent homeland.

During this period, Concha Espina's two oldest sons were married, Ramón to a Rumanian girl and Víctor to his childhood sweetheart from Santander. Josefina had also been planning her wedding when her mother was asked to represent Alfonso XIII on a cultural mission to Cuba. The novelist had already accepted an invitation to lecture as Visiting Professor at Middlebury College in Vermont and a stopover in the Caribbean could be easily arranged. Furthermore, Concha Espina felt extremely grateful to the former Spanish colonies that had contributed to construct a monument in her honor in Santander. Having refused to attend the unveiling of her statue, at which the king himself presided, she could not refuse his request to represent him in Cuba. Josefina postponed her marriage and mother and daughter departed for America.

Concha Espina's reaction to the Caribbean countries and to the United States was mixed. In Cuba, the tropical landscape and the black culture earned her highest praise although she was critical of the dictatorial regime, the less-than-total integration of black Cubans into society and the presence of North American imperialism. In Puerto Rico, with the governor presiding, she publicly decried the use of English as the official language and the implantation of Yankee culture. Her reaction to New York City was negative. The museums, libraries, and universities impressed her favorably but she was quick to notice and deplore the segregation of races. In her two brief stays in the city, Concha Espina felt at home only on the visit to the Hispanic Society, where she was personally escorted by Archer M. Huntington, the famous Hispanist, and among fellow Spaniards permanently or temporarily residing in New York, ranging from important poets such as García Lorca and León Felipe to her former doorman in Madrid, Manuel Ortega.

From New York, the novelist proceeded to Middlebury College where she found the wooded and mountainous surroundings more in keeping with her tastes. Although favorably impressed by the intellectual curiosity of American students at the College, she was critical of their social and moral independence, in which she saw a spiritual and moral void. For the moment, her criticism of the youth in the United States was moderated by her recognition of their healthy curiosity. This tolerance for life styles in basic conflict with her own was later to disappear as a result of the Spanish Civil War. Concha Espina's impressions of her visit to the Americas are included in *Singladuras* [Day's run], published in 1932.

After her return to Spain, the novelist reported on her trip to Alfonso XIII and took advantage of her audience to request the use of the Royal Monastery at El Escorial for Josefina's wedding. It was during this period that her candidacy for the Nobel Prize was

reactivated. Concha Espina received votes from the French
Academy of Language but no support from the corresponding
Spanish body. She was later to learn that she lost the Prize by only
one vote on this occasion.

In 1932, Spain was declared a Republic and Alfonso XIII forced to
leave the country. Initially, the change had little effect on the
novelist's life: 1932 saw the publication of three more of her books and
as late as 1935 she was named to represent the Republican government at the Fourth Centennial Celebration of the Founding of Lima.
In private, however, Concha Espina and her family were increasingly
uneasy about the political situation and after her return from Lima, it
was decided that she and Josefina would be safer in the family house
at Luzmela.

VIII   *The War Years*

Concha Espina arrived in Luzmela in early summer of 1936,
accompanied by her daughter, Josefina's mother-in-law, and two of
the novelist's grandchildren. As in their other visits, they planned to
spend only the summer months away from Madrid. However, with
the outbreak of the Civil War their return to the capital became
impossible. The Santander province remained in Republican control
until August of 1937 and life for the novelist and her family became
increasingly difficult. With two sons actively fighting on the Nationalist side, Concha Espina was immediately marked as a Nationalist
sympathizer. Consequently, her home was the subject of frequent
searches and constant surveillance.

In her publications prior to the war, the novelist's political ideology
is not clearly defined. Although she defended many traditional values
generally associated with conservative politics, she also expressed
strong criticism for the lack of a true Christian spirit in Spanish
Catholicism. She frequently criticized the moneyed classes for their
indifference to the problems confronting Spanish society. With the
outbreak of the war, the latter themes disappeared as Concha Espina
adopted the ideology and rhetoric of the Nationalist cause. Three of
her books based on her personal experience of the war were for the
most part written during her confinement in Luzmela. To avoid
detection by local authorities, she and her daughter carefully buried
each day's work in the garden. Although her writings were not
discovered, the novelist was called before the Chief of Police who
informed her that she was under house arrest. Without food or winter

clothes, the family subsisted on anonymous gifts from local sup-
porters and whatever they could make themselves. According to
Josefina, it was the lack of adequate medical care and the poor diet
that caused her mother's failing eyesight and subsequent blindness.

Although Concha Espina's writings of this period are of little
literary value, their sociological and biographical interest is considerable. *Retaguardia* (translated to English with the same title), *Luna
roja* [Red moon], and *Esclavitud y libertad* [Slavery and liberty]
illustrate the polarization of Spanish society and the absolute adherence to partisan ideology in a country torn by civil war. Whereas in
her previous works, we see a moderately conservative writer with a
strong compassion for human suffering, the Concha Espina of the
wartime novels portrays life in purely ideological terms; Republicans
are presented as mindless animals incapable of noble action while all
Nationalists are exalted as the personification of lofty ideals. The
theme of suffering persists but is applied exclusively to the victims of
Republican violence. Without attempting to pass judgment on the
validity of Concha Espina's beliefs, the intransigence with which they
are expressed and the exclusion of an entire segment of the Spanish
population from her consideration of the human suffering involved
clearly reflect the tragic split in the Spanish society of those years.
When intelligent and sensitive individuals perceive man's inhuman-
ity to man only in terms of political ideology, the violence of the
Spanish Civil War becomes somewhat more understandable.

In addition to its sociological implications, the autobiographical
aspect of *Slavery and Liberty* provides new insights into Concha
Espina's character. This diary in itself attests to her bravery, for its
discovery would have warranted her immediate execution. Similarly,
the novelist's refusal to disguise her political feelings in the presence
of the Chief of Police among others, and her ability to maintain her
spirits and those of her family reveal an admirable strength of
character. The confinement in Luzmela continued until Nationalist
forces took Santander province in August of 1937. Víctor and Luis de
la Serna were among the soldiers who continued on to Luzmela,
where they personally effected the liberation of their mother. At this
time, the novelist was sixty-eight years old and rapidly losing her
eyesight.

IX *The Final Years: Blindness and Continued Literary Activity*

Shortly after the arrival of the Nationalist troops, Concha Espina moved to her son Víctor's home in San Sebastián. In spite of her blindness, the novelist continued to write with the aid of a handmade device to guide her hand along a straight line. As a doctor, her son Luis recommended that she consult a famous eye surgeon in Barcelona. A difficult operation restored her eyesight but the cure was only temporary.

After the war, the novelist's family convinced her to move in with her youngest son since her home had been ransacked during the hostilities. During her last years, Concha Espina added another ten books to her published works. As in earlier years, the quality of her writing is uneven. Age and blindness did not, however, diminish her creativity. *El más fuerte* [The Strongest One] published in 1942, compares favorably to her better novels. In the same year, the novelist was again nominated for the Nobel Prize and again she lost, this time to the Chilean poet Gabriela Mistral. With the publication of *Una novela de amor* [A novel of love] in 1953, Concha Espina's literary career comes to an end. Her final years were spent in Madrid and in her beloved Luzmela. Excluding her blindness, she remained healthy and active to the end, frequently walking in the Retiro Park and often accompanied by grandchildren, great-grandchildren and other youthful admirers. Surrounded by her family as she sat erect in her favorite chair, Concha Espina died peacefully at the age of eighty-six.

CHAPTER 2

The Discovery of a Vocation

I   *A First Book and the Problem of Influences*

CONCHA Espina's early interest in poetry continued during her stay in Chile and in 1904 she published her first book, a collection of poems written during the preceding decade. In spite of her economic difficulties, she was sufficiently confident of her literary talents and her desire to pursue a literary career to underwrite the costs of her first volume. Although *Mis flores* [My flowers] is of relatively minor artistic value, many poems deal with themes which persist in her later novels. *"La mujer"* ["Woman"] reflects her personal disillusionment with marriage and her belief that women of virtue are inescapably condemned to a life of suffering. Here, as in many of her novels, the heroic acceptance of destiny is presented as the key to freedom. Although her attitude toward women is to undergo many changes, her interest in the problem and her conviction that there is no liberation without suffering remains unaltered.

As many critics have noted, literary movements of the period have only a limited effect on Concha Espina's artistic vision. She has been linked with nineteenth-century Regionalism and with the more contemporary Modernism of the early twentieth century but is essentially an independent writer who selectively incorporates influences from the literary groups of the moment without identifying herself with any of them. While Concha Espina's consistent defense of her literary individuality coincides chronologically and temperamentally with similar attitudes expressed by the Generation of 1898, stylistically and ideologically she follows a markedly different path. In contrast to the initial rejection of Spanish history and values by Azorín, Baroja, Unamuno, and others of the period, Concha Espina invariably expresses profound admiration for her heritage, limiting her criticism to those elements perceived to be of foreign origin and destructive of the pure Spanish character. Like some of her contemporaries, she proposes an active exportation of Hispanic values and culture but whereas the Generation of 1898 comes to this position only after a period of violent repudiation of certain "Spanish traits," Concha Espina accepts these from the outset as essential to her vision.

The religious fervor of her early poems[1] and of certain later works is singularly absent in the Generation of 1898. Her attitude toward the Spanish-American War is also very different from the generational view which interprets Spain's military defeat as symptomatic of a more general decadence. In contrast, Concha Espina writes enthusiastically of Spain's "colossal grandeur"[2] and the heroism of her soldiers. In *"Mis anhelos"* ["My desires"], she imagines a day when her infant son will fight for Spain and in "A las madres de los soldados combatientes en Cuba" ["To the mothers of soldiers fighting in Cuba"], she recalls with sorrow the youth who died in battle while at the same time expressing pride in those who heroically gave their lives for the national cause.

In some respects, Concha Espina continues the Regionalism of the Santander novelist, José María de Pereda. Several poems in *My Flowers* evoke the beauty and spirit of her native mountains, and the same landscape predominates in her first three novels. Notwithstanding a lifelong affection for the land of her birth, Concha Espina's regionalism represents only one facet of her production. In contrast to Pereda and his disciples, she continually expands her horizons. Many of her best novels reflect the diversity of man and his surroundings. Furthermore, her view of nature has little in common with Pereda's. The epic grandeur of his descriptions gives way in Concha Espina to a lyrical recording of muted beauty. Like Gustavo Adolfo Bécquer, for whom she expressed great admiration, she prefers the subtle and variable shadings of nature and also like her Romantic predecessor,[3] she focuses on those aspects of the natural world that best reflect her personal vision of life. Thus, in *"Canto de otoño"* ["Autumn Song"], she emphasizes the pale colors and plaintive sounds of Fall, perceived as being in harmony with her own suffering.

The simple lyricism of the poems dedicated to Santander reappears in "Meciendo al nene" ["Rocking the baby"], a moving account of her interaction with her young son. In contrast to the excessively exalted tone of some poems, the physical and emotional warmth of a mother-infant relationship is portrayed with simple elegance. The description of the child's eyelashes softly brushing his mother's cheek condenses in a single detail the tenderness of the bond. Similarly, in "La casa triste" ["The joyless house"], she writes of the death of her young son in a simple, understated style that adds considerably to the emotional impact.

The remaining poems in *My Flowers* are of little interest and on the whole the book represents, as its author admitted, a modest first attempt. She subsequently refused to include it in her *Complete Works*. Although the narrative proved more in keeping with her talents, Concha Espina remains a poet in many respects. According to Gerardo Diego, the lyrical element never disappears from her work[4] and as José Gerardo Manrique de Lara has noted, metaphor and rhythm are but two of the poetic devices that later characterize her prose.[5]

II   *From Mazcuerras to Luzmela*

Well before Concha Espina moved to Madrid, she had completed her first novel. Written during the difficult years in Cabezón de la Sal, *La niña de Luzmela* [The girl from Luzmela] reveals the dependence of the inexperienced writer on the novelistic movements of the late nineteenth century.[6] She naturally chooses a familiar setting for her early novels; Mazcuerras is rebaptized more poetically as Luzmela in memory of Concha Espina's brother-in-law and his ill-fated love for a Chilean woman named Luzmela. The opening passages of *The Girl from Luzmela* successfully create a climate of suspense, maintained throughout in the manner of the serialized, melodramatic novel of the period, known in Spanish as the *folletín*. Concha Espina appropriates their much-repeated theme of illegitimacy and mysterious parental origins. Her plot proceeds along familiar lines with its presentation of initial happiness followed by externally imposed suffering and eventual salvation effected by the hero.

The initial chapters introduce the principal characters and lay the foundation for the ensuing conflict. As the oldest son of the primary landowning family in Luzmela, Manuel de la Torre y Roldán had inherited both the wealth and the mental disorders of his ancestors. Following a period of youthful dissipation, Manuel enjoyed a brief but happy marriage. With his wife's death, he returned to Madrid and reverted to his previous habits. During this time, he seduced a young married woman who later gave birth to his daughter Carmen. When Carmen's mother died, Manuel brought the three-year-old child to Luzmela.

Initially responding to a sense of moral obligation, Manuel soon discovers that his daughter has become the central figure in his life. Unable to legally recognize her without revealing the moral and social disgrace of her deceased mother, he becomes increasingly fearful that his death will leave Carmen financially and emotionally destitute. Unsure of the moral character of his sister Rebeca, Manuel draws up an elaborate will which appoints Rebeca as Carmen's guardian but divides his inheritance equally between Carmen and Salvador Fernández, the illegitimate son of a local country woman whom Manuel has educated as his own son. According to local gossip Manuel is in fact Salvador's father but while drawing up his will, Manuel assures his protegé that there is no bond of kinship between them. Consequently, Salvador's ties to Carmen are moral rather than consanguineous. Appealing to Salvador's sense of honor, Manuel extracts his pledge to assume Carmen's legal custody should Rebeca prove unfit.

Although both Rita, Manuel's housekeeper, and Salvador have heard reports of Rebeca's eccentricity, neither is able to judge her moral character. This remains an enigma for all but Carmen, who intuitively senses her aunt's hostility. Anxious to comply with what she perceives to be her father's wishes, Carmen silences her fears until the imminence of Manuel's death compels her to confess her true feelings. Unable to speak, Manuel painfully discovers the accuracy of his daughter's judgment as he helplessly observes the cruelty with which Rebeca banishes Carmen from his bedside and harshly rebukes her for choking a dying man with embraces. With Manuel's death, the thirteen-year-old Carmen is moved to Rebeca's home in Rucanto, a nearby village. Carmen now finds herself in totally alien surroundings, victimized by her money hungry aunt and her four deranged cousins.

The second part of the novel, which begins when Carmen is seventeen, succinctly but thoroughly describes the events of the intervening years. Although the benefits of her guardianship fall far short of Rebeca's hopes, they are sufficient to check the family's economic decline, brought on by Rebeca's deceased husband. Consequently, Carmen's presence is grudgingly accepted and Rebeca carefully conceals her hostility from public scrutiny. Irresolute and naive, Salvador's initial attempts to assess the situation are inconclusive. Thoroughly guileless, Carmen herself is unable to fully appreciate the malevolence of her relatives; passively, she submits to their abuse believing that she has somehow warranted it.

While Rebeca on occasion tempers her cruel treatment of her ward, the children maintain a consistently hostile attitude. Julio, the youngest son, is the most obviously deranged member of the family. When the atmosphere appears to be relatively cordial, he retires to his room where he can be heard talking to himself or moaning with pain. However, at the first sign of discord, he abandons his self-imposed isolation to gleefully witness the scene from a vantage point that gives him full view of the facial expressions of those involved. Avoiding direct contact with Carmen, he derives a perverse pleasure from her suffering.

As the only daughter, Narcisa occupies a privileged position which she exploits to her advantage. At the age of twenty-five, with no marital prospects, she bitterly resents the presence of her young, beautiful, and wealthy cousin. Like her mother, she continually berates Carmen for believing that she is Manuel's daughter and usurping the money that rightfully belongs to others. Narcisa's resentment is somewhat abated when Carmen agrees to promote her marriage to Salvador. The ludicrous proposal introduces a brief moment of levity in Carmen's life, followed by renewed suffering. Although Carmen relays Salvador's rejection with consummate diplomacy, Narcisa's animosity becomes increasingly vindictive.

Initially, Carmen interacts little with Andrés, Rebeca's perennially drunk and brutal second son who spends most of his time in the mountains. Returning only to collect money, Andrés has ignored Carmen until a family argument causes him to notice her. For the moment, his lascivious intentions are frustrated by the visit of his older brother Fernando. In contrast to the immediately perceptible malevolence of the others, Fernando's character is revealed slowly in the course of the novel. Worldly but not entirely cynical, he finds himself irresistibly attracted to Carmen's innocence. Fernando easily gains his cousin's affection but he makes no attempt to abuse her trust. While his treatment of Carmen remains consistently respectful and generous, Fernando's relations with the rest of the household reveal a moral ambiguity that undermines the initially favorable impression. He observes Andrés' lascivious interest in Carmen somewhat indifferently and although he berates the family for their treatment of Carmen, he consciously encourages Narcisa's jealousy—and consequently her cruelty toward her cousin—with his purchases of gifts and clothing for Carmen.

Fernando confesses his weakness of character on several occasions as well as his conviction that he is unworthy of Carmen's love. The rare but convincing combination of cynicism and altruism culminates in Fernando's desertion of Carmen. He is cruel but also selfless in his renunciation of a woman he loves as much as he is capable of the feeling. Recognizing his inability to offer Carmen the constant affection he has sworn her, he prefers to abandon her and her considerable fortune rather than contribute to her unhappiness. Typically, his noble actions accompany contemptible ones for as Carmen soon discovers, Fernando escapes with the family savings.

With Fernando's departure, Carmen is left totally defenseless, for Salvador has also left abruptly on a trip to France, motivated in great part by his as yet unconfessed love for Carmen and his resentment of her affection for Fernando. By strange coincidence, in the typical manner of the *folletín*, Salvador and Fernando are traveling on the same boat. After learning the truth of Carmen's situation and now fully aware of his feelings for her, Salvador returns with every intention of transferring Carmen to Luzmela. However, in his absence, Carmen has consulted a priest who gives her a copy of the *Imitation of Christ* by Thomas à Kempis. Convinced that happiness is illusory, Carmen readily accepts the ascetic practices of the saint and when Salvador arrives, she refuses to abandon Rucanto or the suffering which she sees as divinely ordained.

In the third part of the novel, Carmen's ascetism provokes an alarming deterioration of her mental and physical health. Increasingly drawn to the more sordid aspects of life, she lapses into an indifference that impedes her understanding of the dangers facing her. Having discovered Andrés' interest in his cousin, Narcisa plies him with liquor and leads him to where Carmen is reading alone in the garret. Carmen's terror enables her to repulse the drunken Andrés but Narcisa perversely locks the doors to ensure her revenge. Poised on the windowsill, Carmen is prepared to jump when Rebeca interrupts the attempted rape. She frees the half-crazed Carmen who disappears from Rucanto only to be returned by a well intentioned shepherd. The suspense continues while the shepherd delays informing Salvador, who immediately proceeds to Rucanto to energetically take command of the situation. With Salvador's arrival, the forces of good triumph over the forces of evil and in the closing chapter, the moral victory is accompanied by the romantic union of Carmen and Salvador.

In his analysis of *The Girl From Luzmela*, Eugenio de Nora correctly classifies the novel as a fusion of three distinct narrative forms: the *folletín*, the moralistic novel, and the *novela rosa*—a sentimental, idealized love story.[7] From the *folletín* Concha Espina adopts the element of suspense, the frequent use of coincidence, and the general subordination of character development to the construction of a complex plot—in contrast to many of her later novels where the plot occupies a secondary position and at times disappears almost entirely. Following in the tradition of the moralistic narrative, the characters in *The Girl from Luzmela* fall neatly into two categories: evil and virtuous. With the exception of Fernando, no attempt is made to reflect the ambiguities of human personality although the portrayal of evil is superior to the conventional villain of commercially oriented literature. As representatives of virtue, Carmen and Salvador share the one-dimensional characterization of their malevolent counterparts. While this simplified representation of human psychology does not detract from the enjoyable reading of the novel— given that it is accepted as romanticized diversion—it differs from Concha Espina's later view of human nature as essentially mysterious and unpredictable.

For many critics, Carmen typifies Concha Espina's women protagonists. However, Carmen's experience of life as well as her reaction to it are markedly different. Her tragedy hinges on externally imposed conditions which lead her to temporarily embrace suffering. As the novelist comments on several occasions, her passive resignation implies a rejection of the beauty of life as incompatible with moral perfection. Like Saint Teresa of Avila, Concha Espina stresses that spiritual and moral values cannot supersede our human condition; they must enable us to confront our reality without denying it, enhancing our appreciation of life and our ability to enjoy it. In this respect Carmen's asceticism is clearly deficient and should be distinguished from the constructive self-denial presented in other novels. Possibly because she herself has not yet fully come to terms with the need for women to transform their inevitable suffering into a positive experience of life, Concha Espina sidesteps the issue in this first novel, creating a character whose suffering depends on external obstacles eventually circumvented. Thus the optimistic ending to *The Girl from Luzmela* reflects the lack of a fully elaborated vision in the developing novelist.

Stylistically, the novel often anticipates the elegant and efficient prose characteristic of Concha Espina's art. However, the use of dialogue is at times stilted and the descriptions of nature compare unfavorably to those of the later novels. In *The Girl from Luzmela*, the natural elements appear principally to illuminate emotional states of the main characters[8] already apparent to the reader. This symbolic use of nature never entirely disappears from Concha Espina's writing although it generally accompanies a view of nature as a force independent of moralistic and sentimental overtones. At this point, the novelist follows the *folletín* with its use of nature descriptions as a function of plot. Thus, Fernando's arrival and his profession of love coincide with spring while Carmen's abandonment and period of renunciation transpire in the cold, dreary winter of Cantabria. As might be expected, Salvador's rescue and Carmen's return to Luzmela take place in an April setting.

As a first novel, *The Girl from Luzmela* naturally reflects the inexperience of its author. Having stressed its weaknesses will facilitate a better understanding of Concha Espina's later literary development and of the obstacles that she successfully overcomes in the creation of a personal style. To state—as many critics have[9]—that *The Girl from Luzmela* ranks among Concha Espina's best novels is ultimately to underrate her merit as a novelist, suggesting that her years of creative activity add little to the quality of her work, as if her accomplishments were the result of an intuitive predisposition rather than the product of a neverending battle with the limitations of her craft. Clearly, both intuition and professional expertise are at work, although in Concha Espina's case, the latter has been generally underestimated.

Unfortunately, many critics of her early works approach it with certain expectations concerning "feminine" literature and choose to praise those aspects that coincide with their preconceptions: sentimentalism, moral conservatism, and literary traditionalism. The same individuals who criticize Emilia Pardon Bazán for "writing like a man" applaud Concha Espina for "writing like a woman," thereby encouraging a sentimental moralism which in the long run proves detrimental to her art. Concha Espina's best novels are those in which the one-dimensional view of life and character gives way to a broader representation of reality. These, however, were not always favorably received by the critics of the time, and she consequently does not exploit her advances to the degree that the artistic quality warrants. Notwithstanding the opinions of her principal critics, the elements which characterize her better writing are present only in embryonic form in *The Girl from Luzmela*, and the novel's strong points—the successful creation of an atmosphere of terror in conjunction with the construction of a complex and intriguing plot—are strikingly absent from the bulk of her work.

III   *The Theme of Impossible Love*

The study of virtue in conflict with evil continues in *Despertar para morir* [To wake up and die], although in this second novel, the antagonists are portrayed with more sophistication. The opening chapters are dedicated to a description of the frivolous diversions of Spanish aristocracy at the turn of the century. Constantly seeking new pleasures, the Marchioness of Coronado convinces her affable but feebleminded husband to summer at their country villa in the Cantabrian region. Accompanied by a coterie of equally shallow acquaintances culled from Madrid's upper classes, the Marchioness and her daughters attempt to escape the monotony of their vacuous existence with frequent excursions and social gatherings. With a delightfully ironic tone, Concha Espina describes the trivial conversations revolving around the various and constantly changing love affairs of the younger set.

Like many of the fictional creations of Pérez Galdós, those of *To Wake Up and Die* are frequently characterized by means of pet expressions, gestures or traits which set them apart from the group and at the same time, illuminate the values of the social class. Dispassionate and imperturbable, López responds to even the most inappropriate remarks with a "Perfectly right!" while Pizarro, the inalterable pessimist, negates all affirmations, from the most trivial to the most profound. The differences between the two men are of appearance rather than substance in that both adopt a fixed posture that serves well in a society requiring only the most superficial verbal exchange. Devoid of substance, communication becomes a purely mechanical exercise, varied only by linguistic peculiarities whose principal aim is to conceal the absence of ideas. The high regard for eloquence explains the enthusiastic acceptance of Nenúfar, the poet-in-residence who conceals his mediocrity with Modernistic conventions that duly impress his equally mediocre audience.

Availing herself of a whole range of stereotypes, Concha Espina applies a felicitous combination of humor and social criticism in her description, slowly revealing the more pernicious aspects of a cynical and excessively materialistic society. In a world where the acquisition of wealth takes precedence over moral or spiritual values, marriage inevitably becomes an economic transaction. This is particularly true for Gracián Sobejano, a man of obscure social origins who arrives at the villa with every intention of marrying into wealth. Like Nenúfar, Gracián wins the admiration of the moneyed classes with his oratorical brilliance. Echoing the regenerationist rhetoric prevalent in the years following the loss of Cuba, Gracián poses as an energetic man of action, a Nietzschean superman who combines a keen business sense with a poetic temperament. While the Marquis sees him as a new and admirable force in Spanish society, the Marchioness soon discovers that Gracián's talents are strictly histrionic. For a brief period, he becomes her lover and cynically supplements his modest income with that of his mistress and her easily duped husband. Gracián's affair is only a momentary diversion in his search for a wealthy wife. Although he is initially taken with Eva Guerrero, he quickly sees that her economic situation compares unfavorably to that of Pilar Ensalmo, the virginal, beautiful and wealthy niece of the Coronados.

At this point in the novel, the focus shifts from the larger group to a nucleus of four characters. Gracián's interest in Eva and Pilar serves to bring these two women to the forefront and enables Concha Espina to establish a contrast continued throughout the novel. Eva represents the materialism of contemporary society while Pilar incorporates the traditional moral values that the novelist admires in the Spanish woman. At thirty, Eva is increasingly fearful that marriage may have passed her by. Although her family at one time possessed great wealth, it has gradually disappeared. Like Gracián, Eva's primary goal is to land a marriage partner who will ensure her financial future. As the product of her environment, she views life as a succession of physical pleasures that depend exclusively on tangible goods. Consequently, love is reduced to an instinctive desire for possession. She also believes that a woman counts for nothing once she has lost her physical attractiveness. In contrast, Pilar Ensalmo places little stock in physical pleasures. Singularly indifferent to the constantly changing amorous affairs of the summering aristocrats, she prefers the company of her lifelong friend and poet, Diego Villamor, whose temperament closely matches her own. Like Diego, Pilar lacks experience in life and sees love as an absolute commitment. Pilar's faith in the basic goodness of people and her Romantic dreams of absolute love leave her open to Gracián's advances. Diego simultaneously falls prey to Eva, who envisions a life of fame as the wife of a poet soon to be admitted by Madrid's literary elite. Temporarily blinded to their unsuitable choices of marriage partners, Diego and Pilar experience a brief period of emotional fulfillment while Eva and Gracián remain inwardly detached but outwardly passionate, leaving no doubts that the couples are cruelly mismatched. As in *The Girl from Luzmela,* the change in seasons parallels and symbolizes a change in human destiny; the first killing frost and the low, grim autumnal sky serve as the ominous background for the two weddings.

The second part of the novel resumes the story seven years later and as the reader anticipates, marital happiness has eluded both couples. In a futile attempt to satisfy Eva's ambitions, Diego strays from his promising beginnings to cultivate the more lucrative popular theater which proves incompatible with his talents. His failure as husband-provider is now compounded by his artistic sterility. Hostile and resentful, Eva can only offer reproachful sarcasm to the poet who foolishly handed over his modest inheritance and more importantly, his absolute affection. United only in their love for their son Tristán, the couple suffers the constant reminder of their unfulfilled dreams while they observe an all too apparent decline in his health.

To all outward appearances, Pilar and Gracián have enjoyed a markedly different destiny. Comfortably installed in Madrid's fashionable sector, Pilar lives an isolated life in the company of Lalí, her beautiful and healthy daughter. Pilar's serene demeanor does not, however, reflect personal happiness. Very early in her marriage, she discovers Gracián's frequent infidelity which confirms her growing suspicion of his shallowness. Unlike Eva, Pilar resigns herself to her disillusionment and in her resignation, she finds both consolation and a new conviction that life offers beauty and enjoyment to those who know how to transcend its disappointments. In contrast to Carmen of *The Girl from Luzmela,* Pilar constructs a philosophy that proceeds beyond renunciation.

For the present, Pilar's moral superiority provokes only increased resentment in Eva. Anxious to triumph in some way over her seemingly invincible rival, and at the same time to further humiliate Diego, Eva harbors a desire to seduce Gracián. She now encourages his amorous advances, deferring the consummation of their affair until the two families are settled in their summer homes. For the first time in seven years, Diego and Eva, Pilar and Gracián, as well as the Coronado family, are planning to return to the North. Having at long last freed himself from his sensual passion for Eva, Diego sets to work on a novel in the tradition of his first publications and like his promising first works, the novel is received enthusiastically. Disinterested in financial gain, Diego sells the manuscript in order to send Eva and Tristán North, planning to accompany them briefly before setting out for South America, where he has generous offers from publishers and newspapers.

Indifferent as always to Diego's suffering, Eva views his departure as a first step towards her emancipation. For Eva, poetry is nothing more than sentimental illusion and sentimentality does not lead to happiness. Notwithstanding her materialistic code, Eva is not totally devoid of sensibility. Cruel, proud, and egotistical, she feels a deep love for Tristán which prevents her from falling into Gracián's absolute insensitivity. Whereas Pilar's characterization remains stable throughout the novel, in the third part Eva's undergoes a dramatic but convincing revision.

Gracián and Eva's open flirtation parallels Pilar and Diego's discovery of their long sublimated love. Morally opposed to adultery, Pilar convinces Diego to return to Madrid and accept her love as a never-to-be-realized ideal. Paradoxically, Diego's departure inhibits Gracián's pursuit of Eva, whose conquest has now lost the element of challenge. Gracián's disinterest on the heels of Diego's abrupt departure shatters Eva's self-confidence and intensifies her fears that age is diminishing her appeal. Terrified at the specter of old age, she turns to the mirror for reassurance. Her obsession with physical beauty borders on the neurotic, expressing itself in dreams where she appears with wrinkled skin, white hair, and eyes the color of death. In a magnificently described scene, Eva awakes and runs hysterically to a mirror, screaming in horror that she is blind when the mirror reflects only the darkness of the night.

Scorned by Gracián and abandoned by Diego, Eva clings desperately to Tristán, embracing him until he cries with pain. When Diego returns, hoping in vain to extract some concession from Pilar, Eva—still unaware of their love—greets her husband with a violent tirade that propels her terrified son into Diego's arms. Eva's struggle to wrest Tristán from Diego precipitates a high fever in the boy which subsequently leads to fatal meningitis. With Tristán's death, Eva realizes that she has lost everything. She humbly accepts Diego's confession of love for Pilar and comes to understand that suffering is the only road to a full comprehension as well as appreciation of life. Following Diego's departure for Argentina, Eva rejects Gracián's overtures with repugnance. With every hope of recovering Diego's love, she decides to join him at the train station, from where they can proceed to America and a new life. On foot, Eva sets out in a driving storm and while crossing a swollen creek, falls into the water and drowns. Like Diego and Pilar, she has awakened to love only to die—literally in her case—and symbolically in that of Diego and Pilar. For Pilar, her future life will be devoted to Lali and to the memory of Diego. As the train carrying Diego passes out of the valley, Pilar locks herself in her room, deaf to Gracián's knocks and his futile attempts to reassert his marital rights.

Concha Espina has been faulted for her overt judgment of her characters, a practice particularly noticeable in those novels which convey a moral message. While emphasis on moral values does not necessarily interfere with a creative representation of reality, it frequently implies the subordination of character development to the exposition of a predetermined view of life. Most novelists begin with a more or less coherent plan corresponding to a more or less defined outlook. It is only when the reader perceives the authorial statement as the determining factor in the formation of the characters that artistic quality is lost. Although Eva, Pilar, and Diego arrive at a similar understanding of life, the acquisition of this understanding differs greatly. The fact that Diego and Pilar remain generally unaltered by the drastic changes in their lives diminishes their effectiveness. Their final renunciation is seen as predetermined by their erroneous choice of marriage partners, a choice not sufficiently explained to warrant the suspension of disbelief. Pilar's naiveté does not fully justify her abrupt surrender to Gracián, whose glaring defects have been repeatedly stressed by the author. The discussion of Diego's inexperience with women follows the description of his precipitous infatuation with Eva, when the reader has already questioned the plausibility of the development. In both cases, the attempt to shed light on the origins of the tragic mismatch are inadequate to offset the impression of a predetermined set of circumstances.

The same cannot be said with respect to the portrait of Eva. She too serves to expound the author's vision but her ultimate adoption of the philosophy of suffering follows a well-structured evolution. In conjunction with the excellent presentation of a decadent aristocracy, Eva's characterization represents a significant advance in Concha Espina's fiction. As already indicated, the vision of life expressed in *To Wake Up and Die* continues in many respects that of the preceding novel, although suffering becomes a positive experience enabling the individual to arrive at a deeper appreciation for life. Similarly, the style of *To Wake Up and Die* represents both a continuation and a modification. The often belabored expression persists alongside a delightfully ironic tone that predominates in the early pages.

Whereas the descriptions of nature in *The Girl from Luzmela* rarely convey information not already expressed overtly by the novelist, in

To Wake Up and Die the use of nature is designed to mask the author's presence. When Pilar's principles triumph over her love for Diego, the moon is described as having a surprised, incredulous expression that emphasizes her moral superiority. Similarly, the novelist's condemnation of the aristocracy is expressed via the Cantabrian Sea which seems to bid farewell to the vacationers by spitting arrogantly amidst harsh, accusing gusts of wind. Here, the natural setting both reinforces the thematic content of the novel and enhances the reader's understanding of the characters.

With respect to the use of dialogue, the stylistic advances are less notable. It continues to be employed infrequently and tends to be stilted, particularly in the conversations of Tristán and Lali. In the portraits of Diego, Pilar, and the children, Concha Espina's characterization of innocence betrays the influence of the sentimental literature of the period. Slowly progressing towards literary autonomy, she first abandons the conventional figures of evil but retains the accepted representation of virtue, so that in *To Wake Up and Die*, literary stereotypes coexist with highly individualized creations. Once more, it should be noted that the novelist's movement towards autonomy was not encouraged by the critics of the period. For many of them, the principal merit of the novel lay in her sentimentalized description of the two children and the idealized representation of Pilar. Graciano Martínez concurs with this opinion, criticizing the ironical depiction of the decadent aristocracy as boring and inappropriate. [10] It would seem that irony is not consistent with the prevailing view of "feminine" literature. Coincidentally, those aspects of the novel not favorably received by critics disappear or undergo modification in Concha Espina's subsequent works. Unfortunately, the change is not always artistically sound.

CHAPTER 3

Portraits of the Spanish Woman

I Concha Espina and the "Superwoman"

Agua de nieve, translated to English as *The Woman and the Sea*, initiates a new phase in Concha Espina's production. Although she continues to endorse suffering as a means to full appreciation of life, conflict between good and evil gives way to analysis of the Spanish woman and her search for happiness. Conflict does not disappear completely, but the emphasis falls more on the internal struggle of the central character and less on the opposition of two or more contrasting individuals.

Like Eva Guerrero, Regina de Alcántara proceeds from an egotistical desire for self-gratification to a realization that true happiness emanates not from physical pleasure but from self-denial. As with her predecessor, unfulfilled marital expectations give rise to the moral transformation. Notwithstanding their similarities, Regina and Eva differ greatly in temperament and intellectual formation. Eva's petty materialism bears little relation to Regina's philosophical rationalism, although in both cases the result is an incapacity to give of oneself. Resembling in some respects Baroja's Fernando Ossorio, Unamuno's Augusto Pérez and other creations of the Generation of 1898, Regina suffers from a paralysis of will (abulia) that has its origins in the cultivation of rational powers to the exclusion of the sentimental faculties.

With the exception of occasional visits to Torremar, Regina's father Jaime renounces his paternal responsibilities in favor of a life of travel and emotional detachment. The death of Regina's mother requires a brief return to the family manor. This is only long enough for Jaime to entrust his two children to the care of Eugenia, the faithful governess. Deprived of parental affection, Regina spends her early years in unrestrained exploration of the surrounding terrain. Contact with nature and the deference of her childhood friends contributes to both

39

her physical strength and her imperious character. Although the experience of puberty diminishes Regina's need for physical prowess, it increases her desire to penetrate the mysteries of human nature. Curious and disorientated, she spends two years devouring books in her father's library, proceeding from poetry, novels, and history, to the philosophical treatises of Nietzsche, Schopenhauer, and Renan. Her studies convince her that for those of superior intellect, life is a meaningless conflict in which good and evil are reduced to the subjective experience of pleasure or pain.

The return of Regina's father and his admiration for her precocity fortifies Regina's sense of superiority. This in turn produces a cold disdain for the masses of humanity. Like the members of the Generation of 1898, Concha Espina condemns the misrepresentation of man as a purely rational creature but unlike her contemporaries, she also repudiates the exaltation of "will" as expounded by Schopenhauer and Nietzsche.[1] In her view, both rationalism and voluntarism produce a sterile, insensitive outlook that impedes the expression of sentiment. Will, for Concha Espina, functions primarily as a vehicle for the subjugation of the ego which, in turn, finds fulfillment in the subordination of personal desire to the well-being of others.

For Regina, this conflict between reason, will, and sentiment begins with her adolescence and ends some fifteen years later. Anxious to convert her knowledge into experience, she and her father set out, accompanied by her brother Daniel and governess Eugenia, on the first leg of what is to be a journey of more than ten years. Regina's dominance over the family members is established from the very beginning; she quickly breaks up the long-standing liaison between her father and his French mistress and subsequently assumes full control of the family fortune.

The family travels to Paris, Italy, Germany, Africa, and finally South America. Constantly seeking new experiences, Regina fails to assimilate all but the most superficial impressions. Her travels serve only to exaggerate the sensation of emotional sterility. Emotionally dispassionate in all respects, Regina's relationship with her brother is the only indication of an unexplored reservoir of sensitivity. Frail and sickly, Daniel introduces a note of human suffering in the complacent group and Regina cannot avoid recognizing it. Temporarily immobilized by Daniel's illness, she can no longer evade the painful admission of internal conflict which manifests itself in physical exhaustion and terrifying dreams that Concha Espina describes with surrealistic imagery. The fear of death—as an ironic denial of her philosophy that pleasure is synonymous with good—surfaces in Regina's vision of a cemetery with an enormous cypress tree surrounded by a dense mass of everlasting flowers, each bearing Daniel's anguished face. The subconscious acknowledgment that she too must accept the reality of death is clearly indicated in her entanglement among the flowers.

For the moment, Regina clings to her belief that reason alone can penetrate the mysteries of life. However, the inadequacy of this approach is clearly demonstrated in a dream where she appears with an enormous head that vainly attempts to kneel down and pray for mercy. Having long sublimated the expression of her emotional needs, her prayers are reduced to a mechanical repetition of the Spanish equivalent to "Now I lay me down to sleep." Acutely aware of her incapacity to love, Regina strives to offset her detachment with an impassioned rhetoric that indicates literary inspiration rather than personally experienced emotion. In Germany, she imagines herself the faithful lover of the legendary Roland, although in her own dealings with men she assiduously avoids emotional commitment. Her exaltation of amorous legend is expressed in a "literary" style that differs greatly from the impersonal language employed to describe her constant movement from one tourist site to another.

The unexpected death of her father Jaime intensifies Regina's obsession with death and her attempts to deny its reality. Convinced that her quest for a "superior" mode of existence is futile, she determines to return to Torremar in the hope that marriage will provide some degree of stability to her life. As always, her decision is rational rather than sentimental and consequently, provides no real solution to her conflict. With Daniel's death during the transatlantic trip, Regina's last link to the spontaneous affection of childhood disappears. Turning her back on the past, she arrives in Spain subdued and skeptical but still confident that she can construct a placid, painless existence.

Although the first part of *The Woman and the Sea* would benefit from a more selective use of detail, the apparent lack of a well-constructed plot is appropriate to convey Regina's lack of purpose. Similarly, the stylistic variations are well chosen to reflect her personal oscillation between an authentic if detached response to reality and an insincere imitation of literary models. The loose structure of the novel represents a departure from the more traditional plot construction of Espina's previous works. Like the novels of

Pío Baroja, this work is held together by the presence of the main character. It also resembles Baroja's works in the use of the journey to reveal the psychology of the protagonist.

The remainder of *The Woman and the Sea* is less innovative both in plot development and character presentation. Regina's subsequent evolution follows the pattern established with Eva Guerrero and the focus shifts from Regina to a series of characters who incorporate or illustrate the wisdom of the philosophy of suffering that Regina ultimately embraces. In her desire to establish a contrast between Regina's egotism and the selfless conduct of her antagonists, Concha Espina reverts to an overly polarized view of reality which leads to the creation of one-dimensional figures.

After her return to Torremar, Regina renews her childhood friendship with Carlos and Ana María Ramírez. Carlos soon becomes her most ardent admirer and although Regina encourages his attentions, she is attracted more by the tragic story of his mother Carlota than by Carlos himself. As a child, with her propensity for fantasy, Regina had imagined the sad and beautiful Carlota to be an enchanted princess held captive by a repulsive ogre. The true story, as revealed by Carlos, is sufficiently similar to her childhood version to awaken Regina's interest. More curious than compassionate, Regina continues to live vicariously through literature.

In content and narrative technique, Carlota's story is reminiscent of the *folletín*. As in *The Girl from Luzmela*, and in contrast to *To Wake Up and Die*, Carlota's suffering has its origins in the villainous conduct of a deranged husband rather than in a more subtle and more common insensitivity. According to Carlos's story, some twenty years before Regina's birth Carlota had married Juan Ramírez, a famous biologist. Throughout her marriage, Carlota was subjected to beatings and verbal abuse by her half-crazed husband. Initially, she suffered the beatings rather than bring the dishonor of a legal separation on her two children. Furthermore, Juan's abuse decreased somewhat when he hired Manuel Velasco as his assistant. Coincidentally, Manuel was Carlota's childhood sweetheart. Although Manuel's presence served to moderate Juan's behavior, it gradually exacerbated Carlota's situation as she came to admit her love for Manuel. This discovery and her fear that it might lead to an adulterous liaison precipitated her secret departure to a small convent in France. Having promised Carlota that he would look after her two children, Manuel encouraged his brother Adolfo to marry Ana María.

Thirteen years younger than Manuel, Adolfo is considered the

most desirable "catch" in the area and his engagement to the
daughter of a woman the town believes had fled with an unidentified
lover causes considerable surprise. Regina's return to Torremar
precedes the announcement of the engagement by only a few months
and the news leaves her with mixed feelings. With the belief that no
true friendship is possible between two marriageable women, Regina
receives Ana María's warm welcome with skepticism. Since Regina
sees life as a Darwinian struggle in which superiority is measured in
terms of success, she views Ana María's good fortune as an affront to
her own preeminence. Her first meeting with the handsome, wealthy
Adolfo confirms her suspicion that he is the husband she is seeking.
With little effort she succeeds in breaking up Adolfo's engagement to
Ana María. Very shortly afterwards, Regina and Adolfo are married in
a private, almost furtive ceremony. Driven in part by her competitive
nature and in part by a desperate hope that marriage will infuse
meaning into her life, Regina reasons that self-serving conduct is
justified by the individual obligation to seek personal fulfillment.
Although Adolfo's motives for abandoning Ana María are not
sufficiently clarified, his attempts to penetrate Regina's indifference
are both convincing and moving. Perplexed but hopeful, he tries
vainly to rouse Regina from her depression, unaware that it stems
from the realization that marriage too has proven unsatisfactory. The
news that Ana María was secretly in love with Manuel Velasco and
now plans to marry him with Carlota's blessing leaves Regina
convinced that her victory has been a hollow one.

　　It should be noted that the nature of Regina's suffering is in no way
similar to the petulant vexation of Eva Guerrero. Regina is acutely
aware that her rational dissection of the human experience precludes
the enjoyment of its pleasures, yet she is unable to alter the pattern
which has become part of her character. Intellectually, she knows
that suffering is preferable to the sterility of absolute skepticism, but
without love, she cannot experience pain. In an unexpected meeting
with Carlota, Regina pleads pathetically for guidance and although
she is sincerely convinced by Carlota's insistence on suffering for the
sake of others, Regina cannot yet throw off her arrogant, rationalistic
manner. Still affected by her conversation with Carlota, she adopts an
unusually affectionate tone with Adolfo but in spite of herself, reverts
to her customary irony, implying that it is cowardice and not
inclement weather that prevents him from sailing in their small sloop.
Taking up the challenge, Adolfo departs with only one crew member
and perishes in the cold, beautiful waters that he previously likened

to his wife. Apalled that she does not feel anything more than the cold, rational recognition of her guilt, Regina falls into a deep depression, accompanied by delirium, nausea and vomiting.

Anxious to believe in some superior force that would give meaning to her life, she feels unworthy of consolation and considers herself irremediably condemned to a sterile existence. As in *The Girl from Luzmela*, seasonal changes accompany change in the human condition; as winter gives way to spring, Regina's doctor informs her that she is pregnant. Stunned and then ecstatic, Regina experiences for the first time an emotional outpouring of love and sorrow, of belief and hope. According to S. Millard Rosenberg, Regina's egotism continued unchecked until the discovery of her motherhood softens and enlightens her.[2] While the promise of maternity clearly plays a role in Regina's evolution, her response is more the effect than the cause of her transformation. Without a prior shedding of the rationalistic and voluntaristic philosophies, in conjunction with a profound sense of guilt and worthlessness, the anticipation of a child would have had no meaning. The novel is not an exaltation of motherhood but of sentiment in all its manifestations.

The contrast between reality and literature represents a secondary theme which reappears in subsequent novels. Regina frequently confuses literature with reality; Mercedes Velasco, Manuel's mother, demonstrates a similar tendency. For Concha Espina, life does not offer any easy road to happiness and the avoidance of this truth serves only to prolong unnecessarily its eventual acceptance. Unfortunately, Concha Espina's "realism" has not yet thrown off its dependence on the literary conventions of the *folletín*; all too often, she continues to employ techniques of the very literature she pretends to repudiate.

While there is much that is conventional in *The Woman and the Sea*, it also represents a departure from Concha Espina's literary model. Regina has little in common with the sentimental, idealized heroines typical of a great deal of nineteenth-century literature. Nor is she a continuation of the female villain of Romantic origins. In both philosophy and character, she is a product of the modern age, although the resolution of her conflict is effected along traditional lines. As representatives of Concha Espina's moral creed, Carlota and Ana María lack the depth and interest of the protagonist. However, in contrast to similar figures in previous novels, they appear more firmly rooted in reality. The same is true of Manuel Velasco and as suggested earlier, Adolfo's portrait far surpasses that of any of Espina's previous male characters. The minor characters also demonstrate growing novelistic competence. The figure of Gabriel's fiancée, a now elderly woman who lost her would-be husband to the sea, haunts both Regina and the reader as she reappears in perennial grief throughout the novel, pathetically reliving her loss as a sobbing witness at all the local weddings. The use of the town gossips to comment on novelistic events is also effective, although, as in other aspects of the novel, rigorous selection of detail is wanting.

On balance, *The Woman and the Sea* offers an interesting and well-developed analysis of the Spanish woman in the context of the modern world. While the novelist is not entirely successful in her first study of contemporary woman, the novel represents an important advance towards a moderately feminist, or as Concha Espina would prefer to call it, "feminine," outlook that will reveal itself in some of her later novels. [3]

II *The Women of Maragatería*

At her sister's suggestion, Concha Espina spent a number of months in the Leonese district of Maragatería, an isolated, culturally independent area that traces its origins back to the very beginnings of Spanish history. *La esfinge maragata* [translated to English as *Mariflor*] is based on her observations of Maragatan life. The novel is extremely accurate in its use of the local dialect[4] and its description of the Maragatan people, but is something more than a novel of regional customs. Concha Espina combines the regionalistic vision of the nineteenth century with the regenerationist interest of the Generation of 1898. The final product is a perfect balance of geographical setting, plot development, social analysis, and characterization. The narrative tempo could best be described as "adagio," a rhythm aptly chosen to reflect the timeless, unchanging quality of Maragatan values and customs. Similarly, the choice of protagonist facilitates an in-depth study of Maragatan life.

Although Florinda Salvadores is of Maragatan descent, she spends her childhood in Galicia in a society that differs radically from that of her relatives. Transplanted in late adolescence to the home of her grandmother Dolores, her gradual adaptation to an unknown culture takes the reader deeper and deeper into the tragic world of Maragatería. Once the wealthiest family in the town of Valdecruces, the Salvadores now eke out a poor living on heavily mortgaged lands. Of the thirteen children born to Florinda's grandmother, only two survived: Florinda's father Martín and Isidro. Isidro is sickly and financially inept but the favorite by default when Martín chooses to marry outside the region. With serious monetary losses following his wife's death and the discovery that Dolores has squandered her inheritance in a vain attempt to establish Isidro in Argentina, Martín sets out to save what remains of the family money. He entrusts his daughter to the care of her grandmother and Isidro's wife Ramona.

The opening chapters describe Florinda's journey from the verdant Galician countryside to the arid, desolate lands of her ancestors. Open, curious, and optimistic, Florinda presents a dramatic contrast alongside her coarse, reticent grandmother. As Rogelio Terán—the young novelist who shares their train compartment—observes, Dolores represents the traditional country woman, enslaved to the land and a feudal mentality that time has not altered while Florinda—with her independent, cultured manners—belongs entirely to the modern age. Of similar background and temperament, Florinda and Rogelio quickly pass from casual conversation to an intimate sharing of aspirations. Although Florinda has been promised in marriage to a wealthy Maragatan cousin, she herself views the arrangement with disdain, insisting that the final decision is hers alone. With Rogelio's promise to write and visit, she proceeds to Valdecruces eager to know the land of her father but convinced that her stay will be only a temporary interlude in her placid existence.

Well versed in the history of Maragatería, Florinda soon discovers that its illustrious past is nowhere discernible. Like the members of the Generation of 1898, Concha Espina refers to the grandeur of the past only to contrast it with the misery of the present. If, as Florinda is told, a forest once stood on the banks of a lake, the modern eye observes only scant patches of vegetation in a vast, barren plain. Once heavily travelled by crusaders, gold miners, pilgrims en route to Santiago de Compostela and muleteers, Maragatería has long been abandoned by all but the occasional traveler. Overcome by the desolate terrain, Florinda finds herself increasingly troubled as she approaches the barely visible outlines of the town of Valdescruces, described by the novelist as lying immobile in the darkness like a dead man.

Life in modern Maragatería proves similarly at odds with Florinda's expectations. In this new world, she must give up even her name, which is discarded as too "novel" in a society where women are not to call attention to themselves. As Florinda—rebaptized

Mariflor—discovers, life in Maragatería is a never-ending cycle of emigration and battle for subsistence. While the men leave for more prosperous regions, the women remain to cultivate the impoverished, arid soil, abandoning the fields only to celebrate the annual return of the male population on the Feast of the Assumption. During this brief period in mid-August, the women who have governed the household and struggled valiantly with a wasteland that yields only to their indomitable energy, submit passively to the authority of their husbands, whom they address subserviently as *"vos"*[5] and attend to as returning heroes. Conditioned by a system that defines marriage as an economic transaction, the Maragatan woman expects only marital fidelity and financial support from her husband. She passes through life with neither hope nor desire to alter her lot. Children are conditioned from an early age to value self-denial over emotional fulfillment and deviation from the norm is harshly rebuked as in the case of Mariflor's cousin, Marinela.

Physically and psychologically more delicate than her sister and mother, Marinela secretly dreams of entering the convent of Santa Clara, where she once visited a young novice. Marinela imagines herself dressed in the white habit of the order, growing flowers for the Virgin. This dream offers the only possibility of escape from the harsh existence awaiting her in the fields of Maragatería. Fully aware that the required dowry for admission to the convent is well beyond the family's means, she lapses into a melancholy that perplexes and angers her mother. Marinela's pleas to remain in school, where she delights in flower-making and other delicate crafts, also draws the strong disapproval of Ramona, who realizes with masked sadness that her daughter is destined to a life of physical hardship. Although Mariflor's delicate tastes are similarly derided, they are somewhat more acceptable in view of her background.

The same tolerance is not extended to her friendship with Rogelio Terán which defies both the local customs and the economic interests of the family. Initially unaware that the financial salvation of the Salvadores hinges on her marriage to her cousin Antonio, Mariflor refuses to consider the matter. Even when the local priest and family confidant reveals the imminence of bankruptcy, she retains the hope that the crisis can be averted without sacrificing her personal happiness. Mariflor's decision to request Antonio's financial support, while at the same time informing him of her decision not to marry, coincides with the arrival of a letter from Rogelio requesting support for his marital candidacy from Father Miguel, whom he had known in their years as students. With some misgivings, the priest agrees to receive Rogelio who arrives full of hope and confidence.

Like Don Quijote, with whom he is compared on several occasions, Rogelio's view of reality is based more on fiction than fact and like his predecessor, his self-image is sadly overinflated. As was Regina de Alcántara, he is more attracted by the literary quality of an experience than the underlying human reality. Well informed with respect to the region, Rogelio sees his love for Mariflor as symbolic of a new era in which Maragatería will once more join the historic process common to all of Spain: "Who better than a poet to open the way for the modern currents of culture and mercy and to bring golden fields from the sterile bowels of the desert?" (*OC*, I, 282). From the moment of his entry into Maragatan territory, Rogelio's fantasy is set off in ironic contrast to the harsh realities that surround him.

Both Rogelio and Mariflor defend the pursuit of happiness as a basic right, although Rogelio subconsciously realizes that his economic situation and emotional inconstancy can in no way assure Mariflor's happiness. His self-doubts are, however, less important in his decision to break off their relationship than his discovery that Antonio has withdrawn his marriage offer once informed of Mariflor's impoverished state. The Mariflor of Rogelio's dreams, exalted as unattainable and exotic, now appears as a stock figure in an all-too-common human drama. Although Antonio's rejection leaves Mariflor to marry at will, it also destroys Rogelio's illusions. Unlike Don Quijote, Rogelio lacks both the strength and the vision to pursue his mission even though, for the moment, he refuses to admit that his departure from Maragatería is anything but a temporary retreat.

Mariflor's confidence in his return mitigates her anguish over the deteriorating financial situation of her relatives. With their lands heavily mortgaged and unable to hire help, Ramona and her oldest daughter Olalla struggle heroically to bring in a crop. When their turn arrives to irrigate their lands, mother and daughter set out alone to dig a trench over to the small brook, accompanied only by the almost senile Dolores. In a scene magnificently described by Concha Espina, three generation of Salvadores women work silently under a relentless sun to reach the irrigation ditch before sundown and the end of their allotted time. Stalwart and emotionally desensitized, Ramona digs tirelessly, interrupting her work only to shout at fixed intervals an encouraging "Bear with it, child" to her nearly exhausted but uncomplaining daughter, while the aging grandmother strives pathetically to open a path in the hostile earth to which she has devoted her life. Unable to keep up with her companions, Dolores comes to the tragic realization that her life as a productive human being has terminated (*OC*, I, 315).

The dramatism of the scene is further enhanced by the presence of Uncle Cristóbal, who holds the lien on the lands and watches with perverse pleasure the futile efforts of the three women to somehow stave off his expropriation of the two fields remaining in their possession. Driven by a miser's passion for wealth, his visit is prompted by the news of Mariflor's friendship with Rogelio, which would presumably rule out her marriage to Antonio and any financial support from this quarter. In a chapter appropriately entitled "A Sun of Justice," the ninety-six-year-old Cristóbal taunts the three women with allusions to their misfortune until the heat, in combination with his age, produces a stroke. Terrified and compassionate, the women accompany him in his last moments while Marinela is sent to notify his granddaughter. Characteristically, death in Concha Espina's work is described with violence and almost grotesque distortion; here, as in other scenes in *Mariflor*, the elements of terror and gloom are balanced by a lyrical tone. The portrait of the dying Cristóbal, with his sightless, dislocated pupils, his rasping final breath, and his inert head bouncing in the dust as it falls from Ramona's hands is softened by the description of Olalla's compassion and respect for death as she patiently gathers wild broom to protect Cristóbal's corpse from the flies and the sun.

With Cristóbal's death, the Salvadores' mortgage passes to his son Tirso, who eagerly assumes the wealth he was not permitted to enjoy during his father's life. For the next six months, Antonio offers to meet the payments and promises to repay all debts if Mariflor agrees to marry him. Having initially withdrawn his proposal, Antonio is not prepared for a meeting with Mariflor which she and Father Miguel had arranged. Thoroughly in command of the situation, Mariflor overwhelms her taciturn cousin, accustomed only to the submissive acquiescence of the Maragatan woman. The discovery that Mariflor is in love with an outsider further increases Antonio's interest since his victory becomes a matter of both personal and regional pride.

With increasing pressure from Ramona and her family, no news from Rogelio and discouraging letters from her father, Mariflor's hopes slowly fade. Anxious to earn her happiness through sacrifice, she assumes an increasingly active role in the family affairs, pawning her few possessions to pay for Marinela's medical care. With the sale of her mother's watch, the last link to her childhood disappears and the painful recognition of her situation becomes inevitable.

While the rest of Maragatería prepares for the August festival and the return of the male emigrants, Mariflor prepares to join Ramona and Olalla as hired hands in the fields of their more fortunate neighbors. As Olalla explains the harvesting procedure, Mariflor sadly remembers her father's descriptions: "At one time they sounded like beautiful parables filled with happy symbols and now they stung her body and spirit like omens of misery and enslavement" (*OC*, I, 346). During the following months, Mariflor becomes more and more convinced that Rogelio has abandoned her and that her father has failed to salvage the business in Argentina. When Father Miguel finally delivers a letter from Rogelio in which he retracts his promise of marriage, Mariflor agrees to marry Antonio.

Unlike a number of critics,[6] I do not see the novel as an exaltation of self-sacrifice although I agree with William Drake that Mariflor's ultimate incorporation into Maragatería echoes the principle of tragic fate.[7] Given the circumstances and the setting, her final submission is inevitable, restoring the same sense of order and rightness, of the harmonious resolution of the individual and his surroundings, that is found in the Greek tragedies. This is not to say that Mariflor's evolution reiterates the ideal of self-sacrifice presented in the preceding novels; here the emphasis on the ambivalence of life supersedes any moralistic interpretation.

The belief that women are born to suffer, as expressed by Father Miguel, should be seen not as a statement of novelistic intent but as reflecting a social reality that elicits both admiration and sorrow in the novelist; admiration for the silent strength of the Maragatan women and sorrow at the desensitizing effects of the land and its men. Father Miguel comments that Maragatan resignation to fate is not a question of moral or religious asceticism but of a people's adaptation to their environment. Alternately supportive of Mariflor's romantic illusions and insistent on the validity of self-sacrifice in benefit of the group, the priest comes to realize that in both cases his aspirations unrealistically exalt the human animal as altruistic without recognizing his equally strong propensity for pettiness. Like Rogelio, Father Miguel discovers that noble ideals are quickly shattered when confronted with the harsh realities of human passion. When Antonio refuses any aid without the promise of marriage and the Salvadores women descend on Mariflor like the three Furies to demand her acceptance of the terms, the priest admits to himself with dismay that Mariflor's sacrifice implies her acceptance of a brutal, dehumanizing fate.

Whereas Regina de Alcántara, Pilar Ensalmo, and Eva Guerrero find meaning, strength, and comfort in the glorification of self-sacrifice over physical pleasure, the Maragatan women survive only by repressing the sentiment that endows self-renunciation with meaning. Florinda's resignation to her fate signifies the gradual adoption of sentimental indifference that characterizes her grandmother and aunt. Her submission is presented as inevitable but is also shown to be unjust and lamentable. Order is now restored but it is only the appearance of order, for as Concha writes in the closing lines: "The light of the sun broke through the clouds and feigned a smile in the harsh countenance of the barren plain" (*OC*, I, 363).

Neither a social indictment[8] nor a glorification of self-sacrifice, *Mariflor* is a powerful study of a people's response to their environment. Thus, the plot is not a pretext, as Consuelo Berges considers common in Concha Espina's novels,[9] but an integral part of the vision. Mariflor's evolution reflects on the individual level the adaptation of her people to their surroundings. With a concern for structure and internal unity not evident in her previous novels, Concha Espina proceeds from the principal character outwards to incorporate increasingly wider groups, all of which serve to illuminate the central issue. From Mariflor and her grandmother, the focus moves to Ramona and her children, followed by Father Miguel and his niece and eventually the whole body of Maragatans. As the reader proceeds from the particular to the general, the inevitability of Mariflor's fate as well as its implications become increasingly clear. Whereas in the train, Dolores Salvadores appears to be an anachronistic reminder of another age, in Valdecruces it is Mariflor who represents the dissonant note in a chorus of somber, reserved women. In a society where emotions are kept in tight check, Mariflor's hearty laughter scandalizes Dolores, who gently but firmly reminds her that in Maragatería, it is not proper for women to make noise and as a consequence, draw attention to themselves. With the exception of Marinela, no one comprehends Mariflor's emotional needs and Marinela's understanding is hampered by her own arrested development.

Psychologically closer to her mother than her sister, Olalla is still young enough to retain a dim hope for a change in fate. With no real expectations for emotional happiness, she briefly entertains the possibility of a marriage to Antonio. Characteristically, Olalla's ambition is expressed by a passing brightening of the eyes in a conversation with Mariflor and is immediately followed by a retreat to the illusionless conformity dictated by her upbringing. Reserved but tender, docile yet unflinching in the face of adversity, Olalla typifies the paradoxical character of the Maragatan woman.

In a number of Concha Espina's novels, effective characterization is hampered by the polarization of good and evil or by an excessively sentimental portrayal. In contrast, *Mariflor* reveals an artistically fortuitous balance of restrained compassion and exaltation. There are neither heroes nor villains in the novel, only fallible human beings in subdued battle with their environment. Nor is Ramona merely the ignorant, primitive mother.[10] On the contrary, she is a moving portrait of a woman who feels deeply for her children and yet has been forced by circumstances and cultural conditioning to deny herself and her offspring any expression of affection. Her love for her children is evident and her initially harsh rejection of her sickly, financially inept husband is subsequently modified in a terse but revealing retraction that betrays a tenderness normally silenced but never entirely absent in her severe, embittered character.

While all the characters reflect the collective Maragatan personality, each is portrayed as an individual with a unique set of responses to the shared culture. Taciturn and imperious, in keeping with the male Maragatan prototype, Antonio is nevertheless far from a rigid stereotype. In contrast to his initial inflexibility, his meeting with Mariflor causes a change of attitude conditioning his subsequent actions. In his silent, inexpressive way he is evidently in love with his cousin although incapable of shedding time-honored Maragatan customs in his dealings with her. Like his feminine counterparts, he is a prisoner to a culture that prohibits the manifestation of sentiment. With the possible exception of Uncle Cristóbal, the characters in *Mariflor* display the essential ambivalence of human nature— alternately noble and petty, enlightened and misguided—as well as the conflicting dictates of social versus individual needs. Mariflor's story is essentially that of the struggle between these two forces and the ultimate submission of the individual to the demands of the group.

Although the theme of shattered illusion echoes Concha Espina's personal experience of life,[11] in general she avoids the subjective tone employed in many of her novels, preferring a more impersonal, "objective" point of view. She eliminates the authorial intrusion common to the preceding works and as omniscient narrator, minimizes as much as possible the traces of her presence. The study of customs contributes to the sensation of realism, as in the Regionalistic novels of the preceding generation. Avoiding the idealization of regional character often found in Pereda and Palacio Valdés, Concha Espina's portrait is closer to that drawn by Emilia Pardo Bazán.

Notwithstanding a number of thematic and structural similarities, *Mariflor* departs from the Regionalistic novels in many ways. Stylistically, Concha Espina is closer to her contemporaries than her predecessors. The expression in *Mariflor* reveals a new interest in concision, in the reduction of subordinate clauses and in the lexical richness of the language. The juxtaposition of lyricism and severity as well as the plasticity of certain images suggest the influence of Impressionism and Modernism. In particular, her description of the pigeon roost reflects a modern sensitivity to the play of light and shadow, the importance of the tactile, auditory and visual impression and the sensation of color and arrested movement. In style as in philosophy and narrative technique, Concha Espina combines certain characteristics of nineteenth-century literary movements with others of the twentieth century. Both modern and traditional, she is sometimes unable to reconcile the pull of two opposing sensibilities and as a consequence, some novels lack internal coherence. Such is not the case with *Mariflor*, where the harmonious amalgamation of diverse elements—contemporary stylistic innovations, regenerationist spirit, and nineteenth century Regionalism—are combined to create a novel that is a modern classic.

III *An Autobiography of Adolescent Sentiment*

With the exception of the young feminine protagonist, Concha Espina's next novel differs radically from *Mariflor*. Written in the first person, *La rosa de los vientos* [The rose of the winds] relates the sentimental autobiography of Soledad Fontenebro during her teenage years. "The rose of the winds" is the nautical term for a circle marked with thirty-two directions into which the horizon is divided. Like the compass needle, Soledad's initial fluctuation gradually disappears as she establishes her proper orientation. Psychologically and socially the fictional counterpart of the novelist, Soledad is the only daughter of *hidalgos* who live comfortably in a Cantabrian manor built by their ancestors.

With the death of her father, emotional security ends abruptly and the happy, carefree Soledad becomes a lonely, melancholic adolescent. Childishly self-centered, Soledad's mother can offer neither guidance nor affection during the crucial years of physical and emotional maturation. Like Regina de Alcántara, Soledad becomes increasingly preoccupied with a need to fully comprehend the mysteries of life although, unlike her predecessor, her orientation is sentimental rather than intellectual. During her period as boarder in a Madrid school, Soledad's rebellious spirit is tempered, but her emotional anxiety persists. The discovery that her mother has remarried causes her to withdraw further into herself. With a romanticized view of reality characteristic of adolescence, Soledad rejects her stepfather as the unworthy usurper of her father's position. However, she simultaneously feels drawn by his warm, sensitive manner. As in *The Woman and the Sea*, the slow, painstaking description of character is followed by the rapid presentation of novelistic action.

Soledad's stepfather, Germán, her childhood nurse, Isabel, and the household administrator, Matilde all represent in differing degrees the frustration of personal happiness that Soledad is so anxious to avoid and from which they are anxious to protect her. Soledad's gradual discovery of the personal suffering that surrounds her undermines her Romantic conception of life and leads her to conclude that human tragedies are not complicated and explosive, as she had imagined, but silent and cruelly ordinary as Matilde had once suggested.

Isabel's sadness stems not from a continued love for the man who seduced and then abandoned her but from a deep shame and fear that her illegitimate son Agustín will suffer the consequences of her "sin." Similarly, Matilde's almost imperceptible disillusionment has its roots in her marriage to a man whose only real vice was his emotional indifference to her superior sensitivity. As often occurs in Concha Espina's work, the description of marital incompatibility remains exasperatingly vague. Matilde's references to her personal tragedy do not allow an adequate understanding of her experience. Nor do they explain her insistence that she is forever destined to observe emotionally satisfying relationships without ever truly participating in them.

Germán's story is equally incomplete. Furthermore, it contradicts one of the major themes of the novel; it validates the romanticized view of reality that *The Rose of the Winds* purports to discredit.[12]

Unable to marry the woman that he loved, for reasons that are not clarified, Germán had originally proposed to Amalia Fontenebro with the hope of providing a home and maternal affection for his own motherless daughter. Although Amalia agreés to the unusual proposal, the marriage never takes place—again, for undisclosed reasons. Years later, following his return from Cuba and the death of his daughter, Germán renews his friendship with the widowed Amalia and marries her primarily because of the strong physical resemblance between Soledad and his own deceased daughter. This extraordinary likeness, the equally remarkable temperamental affinity of Germán and Soledad, and the exalted character of Germán's first passion, revealed in the love letters that Soledad finds, all confirm her view that life is not always an ironic parody of Romantic literature. Influenced by her readings and the confirmation of their applicability to life, she constructs a vague image of the partner who is to fulfill her dreams. She imagines a drama in which she and an unspecified lover are obliged to overcome a series of not-too-insurmountable obstacles before achieving the idyllic union for which they are destined.

It is precisely the absence of "literary" quality that leads Soledad to reject Adolfo Velasco's initial proposal of marriage as disappointingly conventional. The Romantic influence is also responsible for her strong but unrecognized attachment to Agustín. The mysterious circumstance of his illegitimate birth and his heroism in the constant battle with the sea are sufficiently "Romantic" to transform the socially inferior sailor into the ideal lover of her fantasies. When Agustín reveals that his own feelings are grounded not in fiction but in the very real desperation of a man of humble social origins who deeply loves a girl he can never hope to marry, Soledad awakens abruptly to the harsh realities of human sentiment. Agustín's confession of love for her is followed by a suicidal leap from the hillside. This tragedy radically alters Soledad's perception of reality and precipitates her acceptance of what she believes to be a solidly grounded orientation, first in the grateful acceptance of Germán's affection and later, in her revised estimation of Adolfo.

Several critics have suggested a Freudian interpretation for Soledad's relationship with Germán.[13] Although I find this type of analysis inappropriate to Concha Espina's novel, her failure to clearly delineate the psychological formation and motivation of her characters forces the reader to supplement her presentation with theories that would probably surprise and offend her. If the vigorous, direct recreation of Maragatan life appears to be written by a man, as those critics given to sexual stereotyping have asserted,[14] *The Rose of the Winds* corresponds to the "feminine" mode of narration as it has been defined by these same critics. Subjective, sentimental, and illogical, it has been called Concha Espina's best novel,[15] probably because it fulfills the expectations of those who judge her as a woman who writes novels rather than as a novelist who happens to be a woman.

While it is true that *The Rose of the Winds* is the most autobiographical of her novels, autobiographical intent is not synonymous with artistic success and can, as in this case, impede the penetrating appraisal of the human psyche. Soledad's story clearly reflects that of the novelist and was probably inspired by a need to clarify the causes of her own sentimental disillusionment. Soledad's trajectory is thus merely a prologue. Her gradual elaboration of an extraordinary sensitivity and an exalted, almost mystical view of romantic love is presented in conjunction with the much-repeated fear that personal happiness will elude her. Strongly suggesting that Soledad's fate hinges on the selection of an equally sensitive marriage partner, Concha Espina terminates the novel with Soledad's acceptance of Adolfo but fails to shed any light on his character or motives. The novelist's choice of first-person narrator necessarily precludes an "objective" presentation of Adolfo. However, without an adequate understanding of his psychological make up and with no indication of the consequences of their marriage, Soledad's story, as a study of inevitable disillusionment, lacks both meaning and purpose. Unable or unwilling to present the actual experiences that lead to sentimental disappointment, Concha Espina lays the foundations for crisis but fails to provide the concrete details that corroborate her interpretation.

The novel is also deficient if considered simply as a study of individual psychology. Though in any character there is some ambivalence, its presentation must be sufficiently grounded in common human experience to invite the reader's incorporation of the character's attitudes or at least an understanding of these attitudes. While Concha Espina clearly identifies with Soledad's response to reality, she does not make it real for the wider public. Soledad's experience of nature typifies the exclusive communication between novelist and fictional creation. In her autobiographical comments published in *Lecturas*, Concha Espina writes of her almost mystical response to the Cantabrian countryside where she has listened as the sea and the land reveal "their most precious secrets with ineffable seduction."[16] A very similar experience is described in *The Rose of the Winds*. Fascinated by Germán's rather dry description of ants and their social habits, Soledad retreats to a quiet spot in the garden where she is overcome by a sense of mystery, confusion, and passion which is described in a mystical, at times erotic, language. The experience is clearly of importance to the character, who emerges with her cheeks flushed and a new wisdom in her appearance. For the reader, however, the meaning is minimal.

In the context of Concha Espina's life the incident may be significant but viewed in the context of the novel it bears little relation to the preceding paragraphs or to Soledad's subsequent evolution. The problem is not so much, as L. A. Warren puts it, that the novelist has endowed a too-youthful heroine with the wisdom acquired through her own experience,[17] but that she assumes an understanding of the emotional responses of her character without fully delineating the experiences which provoke them. For authors who aspire to create fictional character in their image, the danger is precisely this inability to discriminate between what is common to the human experience in general and what is peculiar to their personal attitudes and experiences. When this discrimination is lost, as it often is in Concha Espina's autobiographically inspired novels, a nonexistent communication is assumed and a reasonable comprehension of the fictional counterpart is possible only in the context of the author's life. Without exception, Concha Espina's best works are those in which the autobiographical impulse is weakest.

CHAPTER 4

Consolidation and Experimentation

I   *The Quijote Theme*

FOLLOWING the publication of *The Rose of the Winds*, Concha Espina temporarily abandons the novel. Between 1916 and 1920 she publishes several volumes of short stories, a prizewinning play and a short study of Cervantes entitled *Mujeres del Quijote* [Women of the Quijote] which was later adopted for use in the secondary schools at the recommendation of Francisco Rodríguez Marín, then director of the National Library. Written in the elegant prose that characterizes her work, the book reflects the ongoing revision in Cervantine criticism during the early years of the twentieth century. Concha Espina rejects the interpretation of the story as a satire of the novels of chivalry and stresses instead the amalgamation of realism and idealism as reflected in the pairing of Sancho Panza and Don Quijote. In that *Women of the Quijote* is less an exercise in literary criticism than a recreation of selected episodes, it is of interest here insofar as it clarifies certain attitudes of the novelist.

Concha Espina measures the value of an individual by the quality of his or her ideal and by the tenacity with which the individual adheres to the ideal. In this sense, she continues the Romantic tradition although she advocates a more harmonious balance of realism and idealism. The Don Quijote of her description does not repudiate his aspirations for a higher order; rather, in the closing pages of the novel, his rejection is limited to the false trappings of chivalry which merely impede the full realization of his mission, that is, to bring about a new order within the context of common experience. This theme appears frequently in Concha Espina's novels and to a large extent, its treatment serves as a measure of her artistic achievement. If in her first novels, the ideal appears with the halo of Romanticism, subsequently she tries to anchor it more firmly in contemporary reality. While her attempt is not always successful, in her best works the interplay between the character's aspirations and his or her environment is effectively presented.

With the exception of Don Quijote, Concha Espina addresses herself exclusively to Cervantes' portrayal of his women characters. Increasingly critical of the modern Spanish woman, she reveals a slow movement towards feminist consciousness that in time will become more vigorous. Her analysis emphasizes those traits of the Renaissance woman which she finds wanting in her contemporary counterpart. Again, Concha Espina expresses her admiration for those women whose pursuit of the ideal is in harmony with the reality of their situation. The perfect woman is at one and the same time Aldonza Lorenzo and Dulcinea de Toboso, carnal and spiritual, strong but gentle, willing to sacrifice herself to the needs of her family but also capable of facing and resisting adversity; in short, she is the Maragatan woman, if her harsh circumstances did not necessitate the abdication of sentiment.

Like many of her contemporaries, Concha Espina was strongly influenced by World War I and its aftermath. The sense of decay that permeated all of Europe during these years intensifies her belief that Spain and its heritage have an important role to play in the urgently needed reconstruction of modern civilization. In a lecture given in Barcelona in 1919, she draws a parallel between Don Quijote's attempts to reconstruct a new order based on the ideals of a previous age and Spain's mission in the postwar period. During the next years, Concha Espina becomes increasingly preoccupied with Spain's relationship with the Western cultures and as a consequence, her perspective expands to include a more diversified setting. The study of character and local customs intensifies as she attempts to define those values and character inherent to Hispanic culture.

II *The Early Collections of Short Stories*

Although Concha Espina had published an occasional short story prior to 1917, she cultivated the genre only sporadically. From 1917 on, it constitutes an important aspect of her work. Whereas the novel as a generic form aspires to capture the dynamic interplay of man and his environment, in the short story—due to spatial limitations—the relationship is generally more static. Psychological evolution is minimized and the emphasis shifts from the individual as a being in process to a single moment or aspect of the individual's experience of life. In both *Ruecas de marfil* [Ivory distaffs] of 1917 and *El príncipe del cantar* [The prince of song] of 1919, Concha Espina employs the short story, with its static, almost atemporal quality, to capture the tragic essence of life.

Frequently the episodes serve only to confirm premonitions of personal suffering presented in the initial pages or paragraphs. Luisa's seemingly excessive terror of the sea in *"Naves del mar"* ["Boats in the sea"] anticipates her death and burial at sea. Similarly, Angela's misfortune in *"La ronda de los galanes"* ["The lover's patrol"] confirms the fears of her dying mother and in *"La suerte"* ["Luck"], Mercedes' foreboding of spiritual and physical poverty becomes a reality when economic reverses precipitate the death of her young husband. In all cases, Concha Espina makes use of a somber but poetic expression to present her fatalistic view of the human predicament. Particularly effective, "Boats in the sea" contrasts the immense ocean and the barren Patagonian landscape with the pathetically fragile steamer and its passengers to convey a sense of impending tragedy.

As she states in the prologue to *Ivory Distaffs*, the collection aspires to reflect the minor, almost trivial tragedies of ordinary life, in particular of life as experienced by women. Although a number of the stories evoke with admiration the suffering female figure who passively conforms to her destiny, in others there is a new note of rebelliousness and an insistence on the right to personal fulfillment. The change appears in *"El jáyón"* ["The foundling"],[1] discussed in a separate section, as well as in *"Talín"* ["Wild canary"] and "The Prince of Song." In all cases, the needs of the characters are resolved in a morally unorthodox but psychologically authentic assertion of personal values.

Like the wild canary for which she is named, Talín enjoys a carefree, independent childhood until a fall during one of her escapades leaves her permanently crippled. When her family relocates in Santander, she is both immobilized and cut off from her native mountains. She dreams of freedom, of renewed contact with nature and eventually of love. Initially drawn to a young aviator by a shared passion for flying, Talín's interest becomes a pressing need for sentimental gratification. Her love for Rafael represents a repudiation of her limitations and is characterized by a disconformity that perplexes her stepmother, Clotilde. In contrast to the self-sacrificing feminine characters of Concha Espina's previous works, with Talín, the author presents a figure who gives meaning to life precisely in her refusal to submit to her destiny.

Forced to choose between a conformity that implies the renunciation of her nature and a rebellious affirmation of her innermost self, Talín chooses physical over psychological death. Her flight in a small plane with Rafael renews the sense of freedom and unity with nature that life can no longer provide her and after screaming her love for the man she knows would never marry her, Talín falls from the plane in what is very probably a suicidal leap. Like a caged wild canary, Talín follows the dictates of her nature, preferring death to imprisonment and the gradual loss of all that constitutes her being.

The same theme appears in a somewhat different form in "The Prince of Song," where a tubercular young woman insists on her right to experience life and love, irrespective of moral considerations. After a passionate affair, she still rebels against death but has at least experienced some degree of fulfillment. Her death now has some meaning since it deprives her of something worth living for. In these and other works of this period, the moralistic overtones of Concha Espina's earlier writing disappear. The characters are presented in terms of human rather than moral conflict and frequently the conflict is resolved in a manner that is morally unorthodox (when judged by the standards espoused in the previous works) but nonetheless appropriate to the individual circumstances.

The change in perspective is reflected in the treatment of natural elements. Whereas previously these echoed the moral judgment of the novelist, in the stories under consideration, the ethical personification disappears. As with Bécquer and Rosalía de Castro, nature both reflects and influences the psychological states of the characters yet remains cooly untouched by the human suffering that it occasions. Talín's injury and later her death are accompanied by lyrical descriptions of an indifferent nature that continues uninterrupted by the girl's tragedy. As in *Mariflor,* a number of stories reflect a growing emphasis on nature as a determining force. In addition, the descriptions of natural phenomena in the two collections stress a greater diversity. Capricious but paradoxically constant, brutal yet magnificent, alternately threatening and reassuring, the physical surroundings acquire a new dimension. Although a fair number of pieces revert to a vague portrayal of character and to the nature descriptions of *The Rose of the Winds,* there is a marked tendency toward greater precision in detail. Similarly, the presentation of external phenomena through the emotional response of the characters persists, but is accompanied by a fuller recreation of these phenomena. Consequently, comprehension of both the objective reality and the subjective response increases.

III   Concha Espina as Dramatist

Much of what has been said about the best of the stories in *Ivory Distaffs* and *The Prince of Song* applies to *The Foundling*. Initially published in *Ivory Distaffs*, Concha Espina subsequently reworked the short story in dramatic form. The play opened in Madrid on the 9th of December, 1918, was received favorably and won the Espinosa Cortina Prize. In the space of a few years, four editions were published and it was made into an opera by Francisco Mignone. Notwithstanding the play's success, its literary merit is—as Gerardo Diego has observed—inferior to that of the story, which should be included among the best of Concha Espina's writings.[2]

In both versions, the action revolves around the tensions occasioned by the adoption of an abandoned baby. After nine years of childless marriage, Marcela and Andrés suddenly find themselves with two sons: Serafín, their own long-awaited child and Jesús, an illegitimate baby whom they generously take in when he is left on their doorstep. Marcela's generosity is all the more admirable in that is it generally suspected that the *jayón* is, in fact, the son of Andrés and the woman to whom he was once engaged. Melancholy and taciturn, like the gloomy haze of his native Cantabria, Andrés had broken off with the temperamentally similar Irene to marry Marcela, a lively, outgoing woman who typifies all that he is not. Characteristically in Espina's work, temperamental incompatibility slowly erodes the relationship and although to all outward appearances, Marcela and Andrés are happy, both are aware of a void in their marriage.

In the original version, Marcela accepts the *jayón* with some reticence, in part due to Andrés' pressure and in part because she sees the sacrifice as a means of giving thanks for her much prayed-for son. Although her motives are not clearly delineated in the play, in both versions her anguish over her husband's probable infidelity is compounded by the discovery that her infant son Serafín is severely hunchbacked. Unable to accept that the offspring of her marriage is marked for early death and destined to suffer the derision of his peers, while the product of an illicit affair enjoys good health and the promise of social acceptance, Marcela secretly determines that her deformed child will subsequently be known as the *jayón*. The switch gives rise to an internal conflict that intensifies over the years. Having chosen to live a lie, Marcela must watch helplessly as her son suffers both physically and emotionally, cheated of his health by a cruel trick of nature and of his rightful inheritance by her own pride. If Marcela has won the respect and admiration of her husband, she has done so at her son's expense.

Furthermore, her lie has created a situation in which the truth of her relationship with Andrés can never be assured. In Andrés' love for the robust Serafín (Jesús), Marcela sees a subconscious admission of his passion for Irene, the boy's biological mother. In his tenderness for Jesús (Serafín), she senses a deep attachment to the woman that he believes to be the hunchback's mother. As the years pass, Marcela finds herself increasingly drawn to Irene who suffers as she does in silent love for a son she cannot recognize as her own. When Andrés and the two boys do not return from a winter excursion to the mountains, the two women pass the night together in silent but sympathetic vigil. The news that Jesús has died in the snow storm convinces Marcela that she can no longer hide the truth. Out of grief but also out of a profound need to live with herself and her reality, Marcela cedes both the healthy *jayón* and Andrés to Irene and abandons the village to join her dead son.

The sense of impending doom and the presence of an indifferent nature, already observed in "Ships in the Sea", reappear in the story version of *The Foundling* while the suggestion of suicide as a means to self-actualization echoes the closing scene of "Wild canary." Like Talín, and Inés of "The Prince of song," Marcela resolves her conflict in a personal, unorthodox assertion of her needs. In his discussion of *The Foundling,* Cansinos Assens suggests a naturalistic, Darwinian interpretation in which natural selection determines the ultimate victory of the fittest.[3] Smith also alludes to a Darwinian influence but feels that Marcela's sacrifice enables her to rise above the temptations of the flesh and purely physiological needs.[4] Although this moralistic depiction of the human condition is characteristic of many of Concha Espina's works, it is generally absent from those of this period. As the novelist herself remarks, she was not attempting to resolve anything in the story, but to present a piece of life. It is not, however, the "slice of life" of Zola and the Naturalists, nor is it, as Cansinos Assens states, a victory of Eve (Irene) over Mary (Marcela)[5] but of Marcela's self-acceptance over self-deception. In *The Foundling*, all are losers to an unjust destiny, as one of the townspeople remarks in the dramatic version (*OC*, II, 956).

Marcela, like all of Concha Espina's women characters is destined to suffer but in the end she finds peace not by resigning herself to her fate but by throwing off the past and embracing a solitary death in order to remain true to herself. More existentialistic than naturalistic, *The Foundling* is a moving study of the human struggle to confront an adverse destiny and to create a meaningful life where fate has denied its meaning. Although the dramatic version incorporates a number of local characters and customs that diffuse the intensity of the conflict, in the original story Concha Espina reduces the action to the bare essentials. The theme of *The Foundling* is hardly new in Concha Espina's writings but the simplicity with which it is presented and the absence of any antagonist create a very real impression of the arbitrariness of life and of inescapable suffering as a basic law of human existence. Here, all are innocent victims of human fallibility and it is the overwhelming sense of powerlessness in the face of destiny in conjunction with the inevitable reestablishment of the natural[6] order that gives the story the serene quality of classical tragedy. Extremely simple both in language and in plot, *The Foundling* should be counted among Concha Espina's best works.

IV   *The Novel of Social Protest*

A chronological analysis of Concha Espina's works reveals the gradual incorporation of ideas and attitudes of little or no importance in her early production. This process reflects the expansion of external influences occasioned by her professional activities and also the general politicizing of Spanish society during these years. The appearance of Communism as a power in world politics, the experience of World War I, and events of the postwar years create a general feeling that nineteenth-century institutions are no longer adequate. In Spain, this period of growing polarization culminates in the Civil War. Still moderate in comparison with the intransigence that characterizes the decade of the thirties, the literature of the twenties reflects the initial division of Spain and its writers into two hostile camps. During this period, Concha Espina aligns herself more with the left than the right in that she moves towards an increasingly critical posture vis-à-vis the contemporary social reality, and her criticism is posited on the premise that change is both necessary and desirable.

El metal de los muertos [The Metal of the Dead] most clearly illustrates her response to the social problems of the preCivil War period. Undoubtedly the most ambitious of her novels, it has been described as a "social epic"[7] and is ranked by most critics as one of her best works, if not the best. It is based on Concha Espina's personal observations of life in the Río Tinto copper mines in the Andalucian province of Huelva. Originally exploited by the Phoenecians and the Romans, in 1873 the mining operation was taken over by the English who acquired perpetual rights to the soil and its minerals. It is this period of British exploitation that Concha Espina depicts in the novel, concentrating primarily on a miners' strike which she places between 1910 and 1920 but also incorporating numerous references to the history of the mines. The initial chapters present a series of characters of diverse geographical and social origin, whose paths eventually converge in Dite, her fictional name for Río Tinto. Significantly, Dite is one of the names for Pluto, the Greek god of hell and death.

Of the principal characters, Aurora and Gabriel Suárez represent the working class while Rosario Garcillán, her brother José Luis, and Aurelio Echea represent a small sector of the bourgeoisie that actively supports the miners' struggle. In contrast to the traditional view of charity espoused in *The Rose of the Winds*, in *The Metal of the Dead* Concha Espina rejects the idea that meaningful change can come from above. In the opening pages, she describes how the canning and salting factories founded by the generosity of Germán Ercilla have long since ceased to benefit the poor fishermen for whom they were designed. Ironically, Charol, a poor vagabond who inspires much compassion in Soledad, is now forced to seek a job in the mines when the monopoly based on Germán's contributions prevents him from selling his fish. Charol's reputation as spokesman for the rights of the poor follows him to the Asturian mine where he is quickly dismissed as a suspected anarchist. Unable to find work, Charol— now known by his legal name, Gabriel Suárez—signs on as a sailor to a British freighter, leaving behind the Cantabrian girl with whom he had hoped to construct a new life.

On the freighter, Gabriel meets Rosario and José Luis Garcillán, two reporters for a Socialist newspaper en route to Dite, where they intend to investigate the miners' working conditions. When the boat lands in Nerva, the Garcilláns join forces with Aurelio Echea, chief organizer of the miners' labor movement. Eschewing the term "socialist," Echea and the Garcilláns espouse a humanitarian system which Concha Espina leaves purposely vague. As the real leader, Echea propounds a return to the early Christian values eroded by modern capitalism. Like the Socialists, he advocates just remuneration and safe working conditions but deemphasizes the theme of class struggle. There is neither hatred nor violence in his vision; he seeks to defeat the Rehtron Mining Company by an appeal to justice and the organization of a strong labor union dedicated to nonviolence.

Temporarily banished from Dite, Echea sends José Luis and Rosario on to the mining town. During their train ride, they pass Gabriel Suárez and Thor, a fellow sailor from the freighter. Both men had failed to board the ship after a night of inebriation in Nerva and now proceed to Dite in search of work. For Gabriel, the journey represents a definitive termination of his seafaring youth. When he learns that the freighter has been sunk by a German torpedo, he becomes inalterably convinced that "destiny is pushing him from the sea to the poison-filled valleys" (*OC*, I, 526). As in *Mariflor*, the character's journey towards a new home is a pretext to describe the changing terrain. In *The Metal of the Dead*, the increasingly sterile surroundings are a product of human avarice, not of geographical or historical accident as in Maragatería. The gas filled air, the absence of vegetation, and the rivers discolored by mineral wastes attest to man's systematic destruction of nature in all but the verdant oasis reserved for the Rehtron administrators and their families.

The miners themselves live in company homes built on the side of the mountain, lacking schools, medical services, and facilities for sewage disposal. Company guards are stationed near all company property and as Thor and Gabriel soon discover, the miners' shifts are long and the pay minimal. While many miners exhibit the brutalizing effect of their environment, others display a simple dignity enabling them to continue their struggle for personal and collective improvement. Avoiding simplistic portrayal, Concha Espina introduces a large number of characters who range from animalistic local prostitutes to the long-suffering but perennially activist Vicente Rubio. In forty years as a miner, he has seen his son killed in a cave-in, his neighbors mutilated by unsafe machinery, and his participation in the labor movement repeatedly punished by imprisonments, fines, and layoffs. Without resources, Vicente opens his home to Thor and

Gabriel, dressing them in his dead son's clothing and initiating them to the worker's struggle.

Like many characters in the novel, Vicente is somewhat stylized. There is, as Eugenio de Nora points out,[8] a reminiscence of the serialized novel in Concha Espina's tendency to complicate the main plot with somewhat involved subplots of an amorous type. This is probably out of her desire to establish personal relationships between the many characters who appear in the novel. In characterization, however, *The Metal of the Dead* is closer to the epic than the *folletín*. As in the epic, passions, ideas, and individuals are slightly larger than life to better capture their essential qualities. At the same time, the characters are profoundly human. Both in her treatment of the administrators and of the miners, Concha Espina consistently points out the fusion of virtue and vice within the group and within the individual. Even Jacobo Pmip, the unscrupulous, hypocritical official in charge of labor-management relations, is shown to have self-doubts although his drive for economic success clearly overrides any moral qualms.

Casilda, Vicente Rubio's daughter, typifies the use of character to embody a fundamental human trait as developed and expressed in the context of her situation. Having witnessed the slow deterioration of her mother and the physical as well as mental abuse of her sister by a brutal husband, Casilda rebels against a future that can offer nothing but suffering. On the individual level, her insistence on emotional gratification parallels the miners' call for social justice. Driven by a passion for Gabriel, she vigorously pursues his affection in a frantic effort to wrench a positive experience from an otherwise pleasureless existence. When she is unable to prevent the arrival of Aurora, Gabriel's Cantabrian lover, Casilda cedes to the sexual demands of a spurned suitor in a moment of jealousy. Bitter and rebellious, she tries to kill Aurora but succeeds only in fatally wounding Gabriel and Aurora's infant daughter.

Having spent her passion, Casilda withdraws into an indifference that leads eventually to acceptance of the same fate she had initially rejected. After her father's death, brought on by her public dishonor and the company's punitive measures for his participation in the strike, Casilda retreats to the now abandoned family home where she passively surrenders to Thor, the herculean sailor who embodies the instinctive, uncomprehending impulses of the noble savage. Casilda's submission parallels the collective defeat of the miners who move from vigorous resistence in the early stages of their strike to subdued skepticism and finally, the unavoidable acknowledgment that their only recourse is to abandon Dite and seek work in another mine where their life of deprivation will continue with only a modicum of change.

In the struggle between the forces of capitalism and the workers' welfare, the outcome is decidedly in favor of the capitalists. The miners' victories are merely symbolic and gained only at great personal cost. The mines are shut down, with huge losses of revenue. The machinery quickly rusts in the humidity of the caverns; the miners themselves experience a slow starvation that takes its first victims from among the children. With no workers to control them, the underground waters revert to their natural channels, cave-ins result, and many mountainside homes have to be abandoned. In a final symbolic gesture, Aurelio Echea asks Gabriel to go into the collapsing mine and blow up the shaft in which the Rehtron Company had constructed an enormously expensive visitors gallery. Typically, the victory is of little significance while its personal consequences are tremendous. Gabriel's return is highly improbable and the success of his mission assures a new imprisonment for Echea who publicly has sworn to avenge the miners' suffering.

Of necessity, the novel ends inconclusively. Collectively, the miners have attained a fleeting victory which does not compensate for their individual losses. For Echea, Rosario, and those with a strong commitment to and understanding of the political ideals involved, the experience has been a tragic loss but also a prelude to a new order which will prevail in time. However, for Aurora and the great majority of the miners, faith in an abstract political ideal cannot supplant their overwhelming sense of personal failure. It is not clear whether Aurora accepts the sacrifices required of her but it is evident that for the rest of the mining families, the episode has gained them nothing.

This emphasis on the conflict between the individual aspiration for happiness and the collective struggle for justice sets *The Metal of the Dead* apart from other novels with a similar theme. As always in Espina's work, suffering is presented as the fundamental law of human existence, but here the situation is such that the sacrifices far outweigh any possible transformation of life into a meaningful experience. The increasingly rebellious note observed in other works of this period is particularly strong in *The Metal of the Dead*. As in "Wild Canary" and *The Foundling*, conformity with destiny is repudiated while the right to take control of one's own fate is upheld.

The question of rights in itself indicates a change in attitude. Less and less an exponent of a rather limited sector of Spanish society, Concha Espina—at this point in her development—is more concerned with society as a whole than with "the aristocracy of sentiment." For the first time in a novel, her protagonists are drawn from the working classes or from a bourgeoisie that clearly repudiates its class of origin. The change in outlook is similarly evident in her treatment of the social institutions. Although the main target of her criticism is the foreign mining company, the Spanish government is shown to be a willing accomplice in the miners' exploitation. Bought out by Rehtron bribes, both on the national and the local level, the appropriate governmental offices turn a deaf ear to the miners' grievances. It was the Spanish Army that fired without warning on the unarmed miners during a general strike in 1888 and the Spanish Army guards Rehtron holdings during the walkout described in the novel. Although the soldiers' sympathies are with the strikers, their superiors, the politicians and the press tacitly or overtly support the mining company.

Concha Espina's treatment of the Church is even more critical. Although her portrayal of the clergy is not as favorable as some critics would have us believe,[9] prior to *The Metal of the Dead* representatives of the Church are shown to be well-intentioned if at times misdirected. Father Miguel misjudges both Rogelio Terán and the Maragatan people and ultimately increases Mariflor's disillusionment. Similarly well-intentioned, Father José of *The Rose of the Winds* is unable to comprehend Soledad's adolescent anxiety. The clergy in *The Metal of the Dead* show neither the concern nor the commitment to Christian values that characterize Fathers Miguel and José. With the exception of a single priest from a distant parish, those in Dite and Nerva have been bought out by the Rehtron Company. For the mining officials and their families, as well as don Facundo, their chaplain, Christianity is not a way of life but a justification of their privileged position. In don Facundo's words, "Christian faith and resignation serve to ease the suffering of the poor, for conformity with fate not only provides happiness in this world but assumes that one will earn eternal happiness in the next" (*OC*, I, 556).

Concha Espina herself espouses a similar philosophy in *To Wake Up and Die* although she never makes of resignation an endorsement of injustice. She now advocates a more active resistence to what she once perceived as an inevitable element of the human condition. Her remarks on *The Metal of the Dead* indicate her purpose in writing was to create a work of justice and art.[10] It is true, as Nicholson and others have pointed out,[11] that the novel presents no clear political ideology but this does not necessarily weaken its effectiveness. Concha Espina's intention was not to show a precise mechanism for righting the injustices described. The novel is a study of conflict between individuals and the socioeconomic forces conditioning their lives. Political considerations are less important than the immediate problem of the miners' rights to safe working conditions and enjoyment of the fruits of their labor. Those who support or oppose the miners are motivated by personal rather than political forces. The Rehtron directors and their subordinates resist any changes that would reduce profits and thus jeopardize their own professional advancement. The miners' demand for greater participation in both profits and policy making is similarly based on concern for their own welfare.

In the confrontation between two irreconcilable groups, the only possible resolution is the victory of the most powerful. If resolution is to be fair, it requires the intervention of a third party. In *The Metal of the Dead,* this role is played by the reader who ultimately must judge the case, not on the basis of political attitudes, but on the principle of human justice. In this sense, Leonardo Erecnis is the character who most fully incorporates the attitudes of the public for whom Concha Espina is writing. His response to the situation is that which most closely parallels that of the reader. Brought into the Rehtron Company as an engineer, Erecnis' commitment to the miners' cause intensifies as his knowledge of their plight increases. Somewhat skeptical of Echea's visionary rhetoric, he is nevertheless persuaded by the justice of his arguments. The exploration of the depths of the mines, normally closed to all but the miners who work there, leaves the engineer with no alternative. Morally, he cannot support the company's policies. Erecnis' slow descent into the blackness of the narrow tunnels where the copper has to be brought out by hand and the air is so filled with poisonous gasses that the workers must leave their work every five or ten minutes to seek the relatively pure air of the upper levels parallels the reader's gradual immersion into the miners' world. Like Erecnis, the reader's response can only be supportive of the miners' demands, irrespective of their political implications.

According to Eugenio de Nora, the novel lacks a definitive final meaning because Concha Espina has no social ideas.[12] On the contrary, the novel's ending dramatically illustrates that in the existing social, economic, and political system, economic expediency prevails over human justice. Over and above the description of the miners' defeat, *The Metal of the Dead* suggests the need and desirability of a system in which priorities are reversed. In a novel defending the working man's right to self-determination, it would be absurd for Concha Espina—as a middle-class novelist—to specify a particular mechanism for the attainment of this goal. Writing primarily for a middle-class public, the question is not how social change is to be effected but why it must be permitted and encouraged.

To this end, Concha Espina emphasizes the ironic contrast between the miners' condition and the values of modern society. Throughout the history of the mines, conditions remained unchanged while the rest of humanity experienced the humanizing influence of Christianity, the Renaissance, the Enlightenment, and the democratization of modern times. A similar contrast is drawn between the natural world and those men whose indifference to all but material interests leads to the systematic destruction of their environment. In Dite's barren surroundings, the only beauty remaining is found in the ancient rocks that defy man's destructive impulse. Imbedded in the massive stones that line the tunnels, an incredible variety of fossils and minerals graphically illustrate the wonders of nature and provide the only respite from the ongoing scenes of human suffering.

Concha Espina's descriptions of the geological elements are without equal. Adopting a rich and often technical vocabulary, she transforms the inanimate world of stone into a living, amazingly diverse and beautiful creation.[13] Tragically, this beauty has only inspired avarice across the centuries. If this impassive but awe-inspiring subterranean world has up to now remained untouched by the humanistic movements of world history, the underlying message of the novel is that the time has come for a new order, based on human justice and self-determination. Unique in Concha Espina's work, *The Metal of the Dead* represents a significant contribution to the modern Spanish novel. It is, as she proposed, a work of justice and of art. As an historical document, it reflects the attempts of the Spanish middle class to come to grips with the social, economic, and political changes in the years following World War I. As an artistic creation, it is a magnificent portrait of individual aspirations and collective hopes.

CHAPTER 5

The Romantic Tradition in Concha Espina

I Romantic Absolutism and Modern Social Attitudes

A number of the short stories included in *Pastorelas* [Rustic melodies] were written during Concha Espina's years in Cabezón de la Sal[1] while others were written some fifteen years later. The combination of works from her earliest period with others of later composition in a single volume provides a good opportunity to consider the changing character of her art in the intervening years. The themes of renunciation, disillusionment, and suffering typical of her early writing are present in a number of the stories in *Rustic Melodies*. The tone of the book is not, however, uniformly melancholic. In "Autumn Leaves," Concha Espina writes of life as an irreducible duality in which beauty and sadness, light and darkness, disillusionment and fulfillment succeed each other. The tendency to equate Concha Espina's view of life with inevitable suffering and subdued resignation[2] overlooks the fact that many of her later works emphasize the rich diversity of the human experience.

This is particularly true of *Rustic Melodies*, although the genre employed necessarily limits the treatment of life's dualities. Each of the lyrical vignettes of the collection seeks to synthesize an aspect of reality and elicit a correspondingly monochromatic emotional response in the reader. If the individual stories focus on a particular facet of life, taken as a whole the book suggests that differences in character and destiny invalidate any single interpretation of life. Frequently two stories will present conflicting views. The power of prayer and faith are vindicated in *"La ruta blanca"* ["The white road"] and *"Las flores de maravilla"* ["The marvelous flowers"] while in *"El primer naufragio"* ["The first shipwreck"] and *"El rabión"* ["The rapids"] they prove an unequal match to the forces of nature. A similar duality is established with respect to life as a positive or negative experience. In *"El azor"* ["The goshawk"], the fall of this magnificent bird of prey to a hunter's bullet demonstrates to the young protagonist that life is suffering and even the mighty goshawk cannot escape this inexorable law. On the other hand, in *"La sana alegría"* ["Healthy joy"] Ignacio and Clara represent the simple but solid pleasures of human existence. With no romantic ties, their happiness stems from a healthy enjoyment of their work, their youth, and a sense of shared contentment.

Although the view of life as an irreducible duality is common in modern literature, its expression in Concha Espina is more Romantic than modern. Like the Romantics, she states the relative in terms that imply the absolute. Closer to the filtered, subdued expression of Bécquer than to the explosive language of Espronceda, she shares with both a tendency to portray life as a series of conflicting experiences in each of which the individual perceives the present moment as the totality of human experience. It is this view, in conjunction with the theme of shattered ideals, that gives a Romantic savor to many of the stories. On the other hand, a number of the selections fall well outside the Romantic tradition. Once again, Concha Espina bridges the gap between her predecessors and her contemporaries.

"Mal de belleza" [The infirmity of beauty] recounts the almost insignificant tragedy of a woman whose dreams of exalted love and preoccupation with beauty cut her off from the actual experience of life and its pleasures, perhaps more modest than she might have hoped for but eminently more gratifying than illusions which remain forever unfulfilled. The idea that life is to be lived fully reappears in "Autumn Leaves" where the relationship between Concha Espina's increasing social criticism and her changing attitude towards life and suffering becomes somewhat clearer. Immediately after her comments on the need to live life to the utmost she initiates a discussion of poverty, and although she does not explicitly state that economic deprivation precludes the full experience of life—be it positive or negative—she strongly suggests this both in "Autumn Leaves" and other stories.

In *"La bandera roja"* [The red flag], Concha Espina observes with sadness but understanding the animosity of the workers who laboriously construct tunnels for trains that they cannot afford to ride. In *"Eco sombrío"* ["The somber echo"], the struggle for survival proves too much for the young Dolores, who impassively awaits the liberation of death. Life is not really lived by those who suffer the physical and emotional effects of poverty; it is merely endured with no real hope of changing or channeling it into a productive, fulfilling experience. Both the illusion and the experience of happiness are fleeting or nonexistent and the all-consuming fight to simply survive leads inevitably to calloused egotism. For the young bride in *"Unico día"* [The only day], there is no possibility of happiness beyond her wedding day "because in the austere garden of poverty, the roses born of love have a life span as fleeting as the flight of the bird and the star."[3]

Again, in *"Piedras y barro"* [Stones and mud], Concha Espina depicts the desensitizing effects of the struggle for subsistence. The dismay of a young boy over his broken pitcher means nothing to the workers to whom he had generously offered water. Here, as in *The Metal of The Dead*, Concha Espina expresses her criticism of the effects of poverty and at the same time her compassion and understanding of its victims. Insensitivity continues to preoccupy her but in contrast to her early works appears in economic rather than moral terms. This same focus is utilized in her next novel, where she studies the tragic effects of economic forces on the human destiny.

II   *The Economic Factor in the Sentimental Novel*

Most critics agree that *Dulce Nombre* [translated to English as The red beacon] is a novel of mountaineer poverty, but none have commented on an important secondary theme: the conflict between renunciation and affirmation of the impulse for self-realization. The combination of the two themes distinguishes *The Red Beacon* from earlier novels with a similar plot line, leading to a resolution of the sentimental conflict uncharacteristic of the early Concha Espina. Compared to the novels considered thus far, *The Red Beacon* focuses on a single central character with a minimum of secondary complications.

Dulce Nombre, the protagonist, is introduced as a young girl and the story follows her development to early middle age. At sixteen, her vitality, beauty, and idealism have not yet been marred by the struggle for economic survival that exhausts her older friends and relatives. In contrast to *The Metal of the Dead*, poverty in *The Red Beacon* is a result of geographical accident rather than an unjust economic system. Other than Nicolás Hornedo, last heir to the dwindling fortune of Salvador Fernández *(The Girl from Luzmela)*, the only wealth in Luzmela now belongs to Ignacio Malgor, himself once a victim of the stagnant local economy. Forced to emigrate to the

New World in search of a livelihood, like so many of his fellow countrymen, Malgor later returns to his homeland to enjoy his hard-earned wealth.

At forty, Malgor realizes that there is little time left to experience the pleasures that economic deprivation had denied him. Having lost his youth, he finds himself irresistibly attracted to Dulce Nombre's beauty and vitality. Fully aware that she is in love with Manuel Jesús, a young seminarian who abandons his studies for her, Malgor remains convinced that his generosity as well as his deep affection will gradually win the girl's love. Although Martín Rostrío, Dulce Nombre's father, initially insists that his daughter must make the decision of her own accord, the egotism bred by a life of poverty soon surfaces and his tone moves from gentle persuasion to violent demands. The promise of financial security is similarly effective with Encarnación, Manuel Jesús' mother, and with Manuel Jesús himself, who succumbs to Malgor's pressure after considerable resistance, accepting the fact that his marriage to Dulce Nombre can only entrap her in the never-ending cycle of physical labor and poverty that marks life in the village.

Unaware of the motives for Manuel Jesús' sudden departure to Cuba, Dulce Nombre passively agrees to marry Malgor. L. M. Rosenberg attributes the sacrifice of Dulce Nombre's happiness to the selfish brutality occasioned by economic deprivation.[4] However, with the exception of Martín, there is no real evidence of brutality and even in his case, the selfishness has its origins as much in ignorance of the meaning of love as in the calculated imposition of his will over that of his daughter. Neither before nor after Dulce Nombre's marriage to Malgor is there any indication that Martín comprehends his daughter's emotional frustration. For her part, Encarnación realizes belatedly the tragic implications of her intervention and determines to somehow effect the ultimate reconciliation of her son and Dulce Nombre. As indicated earlier, Manuel Jesús is motivated by what he perceives to be an act of generosity rather than by self-serving considerations.

More than poverty, it is the impulse for emotional fulfillment that leads to cruel egotism. When Dulce Nombre's godfather, Nicolás Hornedo, realizes that his affection for his godchild has gradually become an overwhelming passion, he actively encourages Manuel Jesús' departure for Cuba, preferring to see Dulce Nombre locked in an unhappy marriage rather than witness her union with the man of her choice. Ironically, the wedding initiates a long period in which the major characters sublimate their impulses toward self-realization in the hope that passing time will reopen the possibilities for happiness.

For Malgor, there is always the hope that the future will reward him with Dulce Nombre's love. Dulce Nombre also places her faith in time, knowing that Malgor's heart condition will eventually bring about her liberation. Similarly, Encarnación, Manuel Jesús, and Nicolás watch the years go by knowing that Malgor's death will provide a new opportunity to realize their aspirations. When he finally succumbs to a heart attack, Dulce Nombre respectfully prepares his body for burial with a firm conviction that she has fulfilled her moral obligations and has justly earned the happiness that now awaits her.

She discovers, however, that time has not been her ally; her own impulse to finally enjoy the full measure of life now collides with the same drive in María, her strong-willed daughter. While Dulce Nombre awaits Manuel Jesus' arrival, María encounters her mother's former fiancé in Martín's mill, the setting for Dulce Nombre's amorous meeting with Manuel Jesús in happier times. Still envisioning the young girl renounced sixteen years earlier and reticent to reclaim the recently widowed Dulce Nombre, Manuel Jesús abruptly transfers his affection to her daughter. Dulce Nombre's initial disbelief is rapidly displaced by the conviction that her daughter's triumph was inevitable.

Ripe for love after the years of suppression, Dulce Nombre seeks refuge in the still undisclosed but long suspected affection of Nicolás Hornedo. According to Cansinos Assens, Nicolás symbolizes true, serene love;[5] for Rosenberg, the closing pages of the novel suggest the possibility for happiness.[6] Given the neurotic character of Nicolás, this interpretation is questionable. Dulce Nombre's flight to her godfather's manor simply represents the final step in the gradual disintegration of her natural destiny. If she could not love the generous, delicate and constantly devoted Malgor, it is difficult to imagine that she will find happiness with the erratic, brusque, and at times brutally selfish Nicolás. Similarly mismatched, Manuel Jesús and María provide a second example of destiny undone by economic forces and by the consuming drive for self-gratification on María's part. Although Concha Espina's portrayal of María is somewhat schematic, she is evidently a spoiled, demanding young woman with little appreciation or tolerance for that which does not immediately concern and gratify her. As is often the case in Concha Espina's novels, the characters neither know nor comprehend each other and consequently, the promise of romantic happiness is rarely fulfilled.

In part, the attempt to convey this incomplete knowledge of character weakens the novel. Narrative techniques employed in *The Red Beacon* suggest an omniscient author but to a large degree, it is Dulce Nombre's point of view that predominates. Frequently, presentation of the remaining characters reflects her personal changing vision of their behavior and merit. During the various stages of her development, she responds to Nicolás with hostility, compassion, and finally love. As the nature of their relationship changes, Nicolás acquires new dimensions, appearing initially as a calculating egotist, later as a devoted, long-suffering suitor, and finally as a generous, love-worthy refuge. Similarly, María, Martín, and Encarnación are modified according to Dulce Nombre's subjective appraisal of them at the various moments in her life.

If the novel is not read in this manner (i.e., as the protagonist's perceptions), it is replete with contradictions that are artistically unacceptable. Unfortunately, Concha Espina's use of third-person narrative gives no indication that much of the story mirrors a single, limited perspective. Moreover, at times Concha Espina does shift to a more nearly omniscient point of view. At one moment, *The Red Beacon* appears to be a story of Dulce Nombre's sentimental trajectory as told from her personal perspective while at another point, it seems to be based on a more comprehensive vision. The characterization of Nicolás and others is alternately dependent on and independent of Dulce Nombre's appraisal. For the most part, the reader is unable to identify which characteristics correspond to Dulce Nombre's view and which represent the author's more reliable vision.

The reader's comprehension is not facilitated by Espina's failure to clarify Dulce Nombre's character. Like *The Rose of the Winds*, *The Red Beacon* depicts a protagonist whose response to external forces is sentimental rather than logical. The view that sentiment and not reason governs human conduct is perfectly legitimate, but if the reader is to accept sentiment as the determining factor in the character's behavior, he or she must be encouraged to incorporate the emotional states that give rise to this behavior. In the case of Soledad and now Dulce Nombre, we are told what the characters feel, but their feelings are not communicated in a way such as to make us incorporate them as our own. The lack of dialogue and Concha Espina's tendency to describe the emotional states of her characters

rather than recreate them impedes the emotional identification
necessary if Dulce Nombre's sudden change of feeling is not to be
dismissed as authorial manipulation. The same is true with respect to
Manuel Jesús' abrupt switch of allegiance after sixteen years of
absolute fidelity.

Even the most unlikely conduct is plausible given the right context
but in *The Red Beacon*, Concha Espina fails to provide sufficient
contextual support. While the novel is clearly not to be counted
among Concha Espina's best works, as some critics suggest,[7] it is of
interest in terms of her evolving outlook. For the present, she fails to
capture the unpredictable, constantly changing nature of human
personality. However, in time she adopts techniques which communicate this view of character in an artistically satisfactory manner.

III   *Romantic Sentiment in the Short Story*

In 1922 Concha Espina published another collection of short
stories, entitled simply *Cuentos* [Stories]. As she states in the
prologue, the stories attempt to capture random fragments of life and
frequently end inconclusively. Like many of her contemporaries, at
this time in her career she repudiates traditional structure with its
exposition of the action, leading to a marked climax and followed by a
resolution. Instead she favors a more open reproduction of life.
Thematically, the stories deal with the uneventful, prosaic events of
everyday existence. Contemporary life is shown to be a series of
undistinguished, often meaningless episodes in which death and
suffering are the only constants. In contrast to many contemporary
writers, Concha Espina makes no attempt to comprehend this human
experience; neither does she rebel against its injustice. In the
prologue to *Stories* she explains that in her view life is suffering but
she does not consider herself a pessimist. Sustained by her religious
faith, she sometimes sympathizes with those who rebel against an
adverse fate, but never questions the justice or injustice of this
adversity.

In this respect she differs greatly from her Romantic predecessors,
although she shares their tendency to communicate with the reader
on the level of sentiment. It is precisely the sentimental impact of the
various episodes narrated in *Stories* that she aims to capture and for
the most part, the events narrated are merely a pretext to evoke a
compassionate feeling for those who suffer or who are destined to

suffer in the future. Children are often presented as future victims. In "*La promesa*" ["The promise"], a young boy's hopes of supporting his sisters and widowed mother are described in a manner that leaves no doubt as to the inevitability of his failure.

In style, theme, and tone, the selections in *Stories* succeed one another with little variation. Pathos is the dominant note and the language is gentle, often lyrical, with an abundance of affective adjectives. In general, Espina avoids the excesses of the Romantic period, primarily because she presents human suffering as latent rather than existing. A sense of inevitable disillusionment looms over many characters but in *Stories*, she stops short of an analysis of the actual experience. More is alluded than stated which checks a tendency to oversentimentalize, but also weakens the intensity of character portrayal. The lack of stylistic variety, the absence of individualized characters, and the thematic reiteration in *Stories* severely limits the literary interest of the book. Whereas Concha Espina as novelist has moved from an oversimplified, static presentation towards a depiction of life's capricious ambiguity, in the short story she reverts to a single, limited vision.

IV *Autobiographical Notes and Attitudes toward Art*

In 1922, during her stay in Germany, Espina assembled a number of newspaper articles and short stories to be published with the title *Simientes* [Seeds]. Some selections date back to her earliest period as a writer but most had never been published previously. A good many are autobiographical in nature, and a considerable number deal with her views on literature. "*La primera salida*" ["The initial departure"] describes her official entry into the publishing world as a young mother in Chile. Other selections deal with her childhood in Cantabria and her love for her native land. In contrast to the melancholic, suffering Concha Espina described in most of the critical literature, in *Seeds* a more exuberant, vital side appears that is present in her work more often than has been noted. In "*Mis propiedades*" ["My properties"] she points out that the Cantabrian landscape is not all mist and sadness: "We generally say that your beauty is sad, but now I doubt that this is true in any case. I find you happy, I peer out of the window to contemplate you . . . and I could swear that you are laughing heartily" (*OC*, II, 663).

Largely, this change in perspective reflects personal satisfaction with her life and with her accomplishments as a writer. The years of unhappiness during her unfortunate marriage have gradually given way to an extended period of emotional fulfilment so that suffering is seen as but one side of the duality of life. Although she expresses the Romantic belief that suffering creates art, as in the case of Bécquer (OC,II,647), in "My Properties" she states that suffering is not the only path to knowledge of life (*OC*, II, 663). If, as she says in *"La torre del poeta"* ["The tower of the poet"], the artist is a lookout who captures the palpitations of all things from the tower of sentiment,[8] she now holds to a broader view of sentiment, one that includes the joyous as well as the sorrowful aspects of life.

Seeds contains a number of playful articles that criticize contemporary pretensions and customs. Potentially a talented ironist, it is unfortunate that Concha Espina did not cultivate this trait more. Her treatment of the popular fears and expectations associated with the appearance of Halley's Comet is extremely effective and her discussion of the use of Latin in the Parisian drawing rooms also attests to a well-developed sense of irony. Concha Espina herself is the butt of her humor in *"Un día de popularidad"* ["A day of popularity"], in which she gives additional evidence that she recognizes her considerable stature as a public figure. Having achieved a certain name as a writer, she finds herself victimized by a stream of petitioners who generously offer to pay her, sometimes with money, at least once with a chicken, for letters to sweethearts, poems for family occasions, and a variety of "literary" services.

More seriously, with "Adiós, Madrid" ["Farewell, Madrid"] she acknowledges the importance of her move to the capital, without which her literary success would have been all but impossible. The gradual widening of her horizons stems in great part from the intellectual stimuli provided by life in Madrid. Similarly, her changing attitude toward women owes much to her experiences in Madrid and to her travels. As noted in Chapter one, her arrival in the capital coincides with her discovery that as a woman she is legally without rights. Her personal experiences and observations of life in the various provinces visited provide ample evidence of the barriers confronting Spanish women. *Mariflor* represents a first analysis of the problem within a regionalistic context. Concha Espina will deal with the conditions of the professional woman in *La virgen prudente* [The prudent virgin].

Seeds addresses the issue in several essays, the most important of which is *"Las espigas de Ruth"* ["Ruth's wheatshafts"].[9] Temperamentally uncomfortable with the feminist style, Concha Espina is nevertheless in agreement with many feminist ideas. She writes enthusiastically of the prehistoric caves at Cogul in which woman is portrayed not as the slave but the companion of man. With respect to the contemporary situation, her attitude is ambivalent. On the one hand she states that the hour of liberation has not yet arrived and that women as well as other minorities continue in a universal slave camp. On the other hand, she believes that the Spanish woman is exceptionally well endowed to triumph over sexual prejudice and on the individual level, she believes that those who have talent and persevere in their struggle will eventually overcome the legal and social opposition.

In her essay "Ruth's Wheatshafts," as in most pieces included in *Seeds,* optimism is balanced by sorrowful recognition of life's injustices. Throughout the book, Concha Espina adopts a moderate attitude toward her subject matter, be it feminism, changing social patterns or the Cantabrian character. By contrast with her fictional writing, the articles in *Seeds* are written in a more colloquial prose that can be extremely effective. *"Golpes del mar"* ["Heavy seas"] recounts in almost telegraphic style the unexpected rush of water that capriciously washes eleven men to their death in the Cantabrian Sea. With the exception of her closing paragraph, she describes the event with a minimum of subjective commentary, employing the short, terse sentence structure of journalism so that the dramatic impact of the event is not lost to stylistic elaboration.

Consuelo Berges suggests that Concha Espina avoids cacophany at all cost and that in her effort to achieve a harmonious expression, she often sacrifices precision.[10] This preoccupation is not evident in "Heavy Seas" nor in the other nonfictional selections of *Seeds.* It would appear to be a function of Concha Espina's perception of the novel rather than an intrinsic element of her style. The "high novel" as cultivated by Concha Espina requires a lyricism separating its expression from that of ordinary discourse. Unfortunately, at times the desire to elevate language to a higher plane results in a style that is overworked and obscures the subject matter in a profusion of verbal ornamentation. Such is not the case in the best of Espina's novels nor is it true of *Seeds.* The collection offers a wide range of topics and reveals more of Concha Espina's personality than any other single work in her production. It proves that stylistically she is more versatile than a reader of her fiction would suspect. Continuing this vein would have added a new dimension to her writing and it is unfortunate that she did not pursue it further.

V   Bécquer and the Romantic Novel in Concha Espina

Throughout her career, Concha Espina returns repeatedly to the Romantic premise that sentiment is both the origin and medium of artistic expression. Although on occasion she abandons this approach and produces novels that deal primarily with other aspects of life, she invariably reverts to the novel of sentiment. Almost always, these novels revolve around a female protagonist whose dreams of sentimental fulfillment fail to materialize. It is not so much that the aspirations of the heroine are unattainable as that destiny or human error intervene to separate her from the individual with whom she could otherwise realize sentimental fulfillment. In no case is the disparity between the real and the ideal presented as inherent to the human experience; the conflict lies solely in the erroneous pairing of temperamentally disparate individuals, of which at least one suffers in the knowledge that he or she has unwittingly exchanged the assurance of emotional plenitude for a life of emotional deprivation.

This view of sentimental frustration differs considerably from that of the "early" Romantics,[11] whose vision of life revolves around the premise that the ideal is by definition unattainable. Man's capacity to aspire to a higher level leads only to disillusionment as he comes to realize that his perception of what should be is grossly disproportionate to what is. In Bécquer, as in many Romantics, this idea is applied to the aesthetic as well as the sentimental experience; in art as in love, the superior individual is destined to strive continually for the absolute, knowing that its realization is beyond the realm of possibility. Although the certainty of failure gives rise to frustration, and at times desperation, there is also a certain exultation in many of the Romantics, for as Abrams points out, they console themselves with the belief that the measure of one's dignity or greatness is precisely the disparity between one's ideal and one's reality.[12]

In contrast to the novels considered thus far, *El caliz rojo* [The red chalice] is closer to Bécquer than to the *folletín* in its presentation of the protagonist's sentimental dilemma. In the prologue to the novel, Espina remarks that it contains no real action, no external occurrences, no dramatic conflicts; in sum, it is the antithesis of the serialized literature of the period.

Against a rural German backdrop, the novel contrasts the moral and spiritual bankruptcy of post-World War I Germany with the unshakable idealism of Soledad Fontenebro *(The Rose of the Winds)*. Now separated from her husband, Soledad lives in self-imposed banishment with neither hope nor desire for the happiness to which she once aspired. The specific details of her marital break-up are never fully explained and in terms of Soledad's disillusionment, they are irrelevant. Whatever precipitated her flight from the comfortable, bourgeois life with Adolfo Velasco, from her perspective their relationship fell far short of the absolute love which she continues to revere with an almost religious passion. The fact that Soledad rejects any possibility of reconciliation regardless of the conditions confirms that her marital difficulties stem from the disparity between lived reality and the ideal rather than from a specific incident. In her own words, her loss is irremediable because the once invincible love "is no longer exemplary and glorious, burning in the heights like a torch in the heavens; it has been thrown down into an abyss and its grandeur, on disintegrating, covers it with reproaches" *(OC,* I, 704).

Reality has forever interposed itself between Soledad and the ideal, leaving her torn between a sense of irretrievable loss and a need to nurture her dream in solitude. Like the Romantics, she actively cultivates memory, continually rekindling the ashes of her passion. She thereby recreates the acute sense of loss that verifies the reality of her experience and enables her to persist in the cult of absolute love. Soledad not only exemplifies the pursuit of the ideal as portrayed by the Romantics, she herself represents the ideal woman of Romantic literature. To present this facet of her character, Concha Espina introduces the figure of Ismael Davalos, a Sephardic Jew who befriends Soledad during her stay in the Falk See. Like Soledad, he belongs to the "aristocracy of sentiment," in marked contrast to the pleasure seekers who invade the region during the summer months. Well-educated, financially privileged, and one of a group that has suffered centuries of social and political ostracism, Davalos immediately perceives the uncommon sensitivity of his companion. Potentially an interesting character, he is not fully developed as an independent figure, serving primarily to elucidate Soledad's story.

Davalos initially opposes Soledad's idealism, hoping that she will agree to reconstruct a life of happiness with him. Gradually, his admiration for her constancy prevails and in the end, he observes Soledad's departure to the remote Stienitz See with the knowledge that his love for her is inextricably tied to the idealism he once sought to modify. In Davalos' view, Soledad represents the Romantic fusion of art and love. Rephrasing Bécquer's "Poesía . . . eres tú" [Poetry . . . is you], he tells her "You are art made love" (OC, I, 698). Echoing the Romantic belief that suffering provides the medium necessary for the creation of beauty, Soledad is compared to the sandalwood tree which generously perfumes the axe that wounds it.

Ideally, Davalos' gradual conversion to Soledad's cult of absolute love should serve as a vehicle for a similar conversion on the part of the reader. This is not the case and as a consequence, the potential impact of the novel is weakened. It is not so much (as Concha Espina and later Gerardo Diego argue[13]) that the book is intended for a select minority. Nor can it be said that the modern reader is poorly disposed to accept the Romantic sensibility. Bécquer's Romanticism is no less "elitist" and yet he continues to enjoy a reading public that equals, if not surpasses, that of many "popular" writers. The difference is one of artistic quality, not thematic obscurity or disparate sensibilities.

Whereas Bécquer transmits a sense of the ineffable with a language grounded in concrete realities, Espina attempts to capture the sublime with a language excessively vague, both in intellectual content and the emotional implications. Typical of the expression employed in The Red Chalice, the following example obscures rather than clarifies, losing the reader in an imprecision that hinders assimilation of Soledad's emotional state:

> In her avid desire for evasion, she imagines level beaches, where her spirit might be calmed; she accepts a robe of snow and a breeze of ice in order to soothe the ardent suffering. And it could be said that the water of her dreary eyes sinking in the nearness of memory had some contact with the eternal fire of the planet; thus the crystalline murmur of her voice contrasted with the burning obscurity of her pupils. (OC, I, 721)

The assimilation of Soledad's experience is additionally hindered by her dual characterization as the ideal incarnate and the victim of insufficient reality. Soledad's perfection invalidates the premise that human experience is cruelly disproportionate to human aspirations. Her embodiment of the ideal would presumably enable a husband who shared her Romantic vision to attain the absolute experience of love that the novel elsewhere suggests is unattainable.

The frustration of sentimental fulfillment becomes once more a function of temperamental incompatibility rather than of human destiny. Furthermore, the exaltation of Soledad and Davalos as members of an "aristocracy of sentiment" loses force because it is based on racial and national divisions. The arbitrary characterization of the Ashkenazic Jews as coarse and ill-bred (*OC*, I, 696) could be written off as impassioned rhetoric in the mouth of the Sephardic Davalos, but allusions to semiteutonic churlishness and portrayal of the German people as uniformly indifferent to rights and virtues in their hedonistic quest for instant gratification suggests an overly simplistic view of humanity that undermines the novel's credibility.

The chauvinistic note in *The Red Beacon* stems from a growing conviction that Spain and the Spanish-speaking world have an important role to play in the reconstruction of postwar civilization, a facet which, as already mentioned, concurs with the Generation of 1898, as does the general outline of her thinking, although Concha Espina differs in tenor and in the particulars of her ideology. Laín Entralgo points out that following the initial rejection of all things Spanish, the Generation of 1898 moves to a positive reevaluation of the Spanish heritage and character.[14] More moderate in her criticism of Spain and its institutions, Concha Espina later becomes more hyperbolic in her praise. For the present, this tendency does not exclude a critical appraisal of Spanish society; subsequently, the defense of Spain and its culture become the overriding theme of her works.

CHAPTER 6

Spanish Tradition and Contemporary Culture

I   The Two Modes of Literature in Concha Espina

THE comparison of Hispanic values and postwar German society continues in *Tierras del Aquilón* [Lands of the north wind], a collection of short stories and essays based on Concha Espina's trip to Germany. In two of the stories, representatives of the two cultures are directly contrasted. *"Un dólar"* ["One dollar"] presents the materialistic values of Gertrudis, a German woman whose plans to marry a wealthy Latin American coffee grower are motivated solely by financial considerations. Unwilling to learn Spanish, she cultivates the friendship of Carmen, a young Spanish girl who represents spiritual over material values. While translating Gertrudis' letters to the coffee grower, Carmen interjects a note of warmth in the unimpassioned acceptance of marriage and deletes the purposely overestimated requests for travel expenses.

"Erika" shifts emphasis from the contrast between materialism and sentiment to that of self-restraint and the drive for gratification. Erika, a young German girl, and Miguel de Quirós, a young *hidalgo* from Seville, find themselves strongly attracted to each other, but whereas Erika blindly pursues her passion with no thought of moral or social norms, Miguel's love for his Spanish fiancée and his concept of honor enable him to overcome his physical impulses. Although the contrast between German and Spanish values in "One Dollar" and "Erika" is not as extreme as that presented in *The Red Chalice*, it is still excessively simplistic. Concha Espina's tendency to polarize characters or points of view continues, and generally, her art suffers when portraying the contrast between two distinct elements. However, in her best works, opposing forces are presented with no real attempt to resolve their differences or to impose a moral judgment.

This is the case in the remaining two stories in *Lands of the North Wind,* both of which suggest the moral bankruptcy of postwar Germany far more effectively, precisely because the references to Spain's moral "solvency" are absent.

"Aves de paso" ["Migratory birds"] depicts the changing character of German society, introducing characters influenced by the war experience in various ways. Prior to the war, Agata and Dora enjoy a comfortable existence that comes to an abrupt end with the outbreak of hostilities. Intimate friends since childhood, they share the same school experiences, the same customs, even the same first boy friend. The war's end brings the first changes in their destinies. Dora's father returns and the family enters a new era of prosperity while Agata's father dies in prison, leaving his numerous offspring destitute. Agata's only hope now lies with Roger, a young veteran who continues to divide his attentions between the two girls. Indolent and egotistical by nature, Roger falls easy prey to postwar hedonism. Basking in his position of handsome, healthy survivor, he avidly pursues the pleasures denied him during the war. Agata's appeal loses out to Dora's money, and she in turn is abandoned for a wealthier rival. In the end, however, financial security proves less important than the impulse for immediate gratification. Roger escapes to the bohemian life of the *Wandervogel*[1] with Agata's younger sister whose imperious drive for physical enjoyment typifies the mood of war-weary Germany.

A similar theme appears in *"Cristales"* ["Glass window"], in which Annchen, a young German girl, discards the love of Auscar, a poor but devoted suitor, for the material comforts promised by a wealthy banker. Both in "Migratory Birds" and "Glass Window," Concha Espina devotes considerable attention to describing tangible, often sensual, objects that serve to recreate the materialistic character of the atmosphere. Dora's plumpness and her rosy cheeks against the background of her father's well-stocked meat store synthesize the preoccupation with the flesh. In "Glass Window," the language is more Modernistic, blending sensuality and exoticism to emphasize the decadent tenor of society.

Working at a local flower shop, Annchen exhibits herself in the store window, dressed in a Roman tunic which she drapes suggestively over her well-endowed body. Instinctively attuned to all that enhances her beauty, her only ambition is to ensure her financial future by selling herself to the highest bidder. Given her shallow understanding of human needs, Annchen underestimates the force of

Auscar's passion and proceeds with her plans to move into the banker's villa. On the arranged day she leaves the flower shop in the banker's limousine, unaware that Auscar has hired himself out as the banker's chauffeur. In the car, Annchen remains emotionally cool but physically responsive to the banker's passion. Her histrionics are suddenly interrupted by the appearance of Auscar's tormented face when he jumps out of the car from the driver's seat and watches impassively while the still speeding car disappears into a lake. Like the *nemesis* of classical tragedy, Auscar's vengeance represents a return to a higher order, and as in true tragedy, the violent resolution of the action evokes a feeling of justice in the reader. In the end, human sentiment must prevail.

The message, essentially the same in "Erika" and in "Glass Window," emanates from the core of the work in the latter whereas in the former it is imposed on and conditions the artistic representation. Espina clearly understands the nature of tragedy and some of her best works bear the mark of the genre. Influenced by the sentimental literature of her formative years and encouraged by many critics predisposed to accept this facet of her work, she chose not to pursue the classical tragedy in most of her writing. Once again, her choice is not always artistically solid.

II *Covadonga and* Altar Mayor: *Vision of a New Reconquest*

Concha Espina's next novel continues both the polarized presentation of good and evil and the nationalistic tenor of the preceding works. Although *Altar mayor* [High Altar] was favorably received at the time of publication—it was awarded the National Prize for Literature—it is now generally considered an inferior novel. Nora and Gerardo Diego have pointed out that it bears some resemblance to Pereda's novels in its descriptions of landscape, while in terms of plot development, it relies on the melodramatic effects and one-dimensional characters of the *folletín*. [2]

Concha Espina's interest in the region of Covadonga dates back to the early 1920's when she published a short story entitled "*Cumbres al sol*" ["Peaks in the sun"]. In this early version of *High Altar*, she introduces the major characters and establishes the sentimental conflict elaborated along somewhat different lines in the later novel. The story opens with the introduction of Xavier de Escosura, who has been called to Covadonga by his domineering mother to marry the wealthy and aristocratic Leonor Jove. Xavier's trip through Asturias brings back the memory of a visit four years earlier, during which he had sworn before the Virgin of Covadonga to marry his young cousin Teresa. Well-intentioned but weak-willed, Xavier left for San Sebastián, promptly forgot his promise and initiated an affair with a married woman.

The news that Teresa had departed for South America with her married sister serves to ease Xavier's sense of guilt and he proceeds to Covadonga convinced that the unfortunate episode is closed. His discovery that Teresa has in fact chosen to remain in her birthplace leaves him perturbed, but also assured that she has been the only real passion of his life. Notwithstanding Teresa's protests that she can never love or trust him again, Xavier informs his mother that he cannot accept the marriage she has arranged and that he will not rest until he has earned the right to marry Teresa. "Peaks in the Sun" closes inconclusively with this declaration, leaving the reader to choose among several possible endings. In what will later be the first three chapters of *High Altar,* Concha Espina draws a clear picture of the conflicting interpersonal relationships influencing the main characters. Uncharacteristically, the dialogue employed is both abundant and natural; as always, the descriptions of landscape are extremely effective. "Peaks in the Sun" is an excellent little work that has unfortunately been lost in the mass of the longer novel.

With the exception of the descriptive passages, the two works are totally dissimilar. The self-sufficient, tongue-in-cheek Teresa of "Peaks in the Sun" becomes one more example of exalted sentimentality in *High Altar.* Xavier's weakness of character becomes the dominant note of his personality while his mother, Eulalia, acquires the stature of the classical villain. The action in the novel is complicated by the introduction of a number of minor characters who illustrate the division of Spanish society into two distinct groups. Teresa, José—her Asturian suitor—and the local residents represent the true Spanish heritage dating back to the Visigothic reign and the early days of the Reconquest. Intensely patriotic, individualistic, physically strong, instinctively aristocratic, highly religious, and committed to the principles of love, loyalty, and moral rectitude, the Asturian natives stand in marked contrast to the self-indulgent aristocracy of contemporary Spain, represented by Eulalia, Leonor and their companions. Guided by materialistic considerations and a strong sense of social convention, Eulalia employs bribery, calumny, and deceit in what she interprets as her God-given responsibility to assure her son's social and economic security.

Notwithstanding Xavier's genuine love for Teresa and his public declaration of marital intent—accompanied this time by the traditional exchange of engagement rings before the altar of Covadonga—Xavier succumbs to his mother's pressure. The townspeople perceive an act of divine justice when his wedding to Leonor is accompanied by a torrential outburst, and after the ceremony, Leonor falls fatally ill with meningitis. Her death is followed by clearing weather and the safe return of José, who had braved the storm to go for a doctor at Teresa's request. Following the tradition of *To Wake Up and Die,* two couples are tragically mismatched but here, the final pages suggest a possible happy resolution, as Teresa's suffering and José's constancy are rewarded with the promise of bliss in their union.

With the exception of Concha Espina's war novels, *High Altar* is probably the weakest of her works. Although her attitude during the Civil War differs considerably from that expressed in *High Altar,* certain underlying similarities bear noting. The idea of a united Hispanic force, previously expressed in *The Red Chalice,* reappears in *High Altar* in the character Yacub Es-Saheli, a Lebanese Christian who advocates a new Spanish reconquest based on the principles of love and peace. Yacub views Spain as a land in which the blood of many races and peoples has been fused to create a unique type eminently qualified to lead the Hispanic world in the formation of a new culture. His poetic vision is that of science and beauty, progress and humanitarianism, as well as a democratic spirit coexisting in harmonious balance.

Yacub's ideas reflect Espina's personal views and should be related to the nationalistic spirit that arose in Spain and Western Europe during the early twentieth century. In Spain, its roots can be traced back to Menéndez y Pelayo's exaltation of Spanish history, philosophy and character. Later, the Generation of 1898 prolonged the attitude via their insistence on Spanish singularity. The theme persists in Ortega y Gasset as well as in many major and minor writers, politicians, and historians. Throughout Europe, the emphasis on national character is incorporated into the fascist rhetoric of the 1920's and 1930's. Clearly, Ortega y Gasset, Unamuno, Menéndez y Pelayo, Concha Espina and many others who expressed belief in a unique Spanish character are not to be classified as prefascists. While some, including Concha Espina, come to espouse the Falangist cause, others energetically disassociate themselves from the movement. Nevertheless, all reflect in some way the nationalistic spirit of the period.

Concha Espina, like most of her contemporaries, does not construct a clear political or social program. Except for the repeated rejection of violence, Yacub's discussion of the matter is presented in vague allusions to Hispanic values and poetic forecasts of a new world order. It is doubtful that Concha Espina originally intended to write a novel of national exaltation. "Peaks in the Sun" contains little to suggest such a purpose and even in *High Altar*, Jacub does not appear until chapter eleven. Whatever her initial intent, the final product is a panegyric of Hispanic character, a call for the reaffirmation of traditional values. As observed earlier, Espina's work generally suffers when she attempts to contrast two opposing forces. When this polarization is compounded by a strong nationalistic spirit—as in *High Altar*—artistic value is seriously diminished. Excepting the chapters previously published as "Peaks in the Sun," the only positive aspect of the novel is its representation of the natural surroundings, wherein *High Altar* surpasses all but one or two of Concha Espina's works. Covadonga lies in an incredibly varied setting that the novelist captures in all its variations; majestic and lyrical, fearsome and assuring, cloud-enshrouded and sun-streaked. For those who prefer plot or character development to descriptive passages, *High Altar* can offer little; for those who wish to gain some feeling for the incredible beauty of Covadonga and its surroundings, the descriptive passages are invaluable.

III   A Balancing of Dualities

Characteristically, a narrowing of perspecitve in Concha Espina's writing is followed as if rhythmically by a sudden breadth of vision. In contrast to the one-dimensional characters and the equally restricted ideology of *High Altar*, the three stories included in *Llama de cera* [Wax flame] illustrate once more the irreducible duality of life. Originally published in 1925 with the title *"El secreto de un disfraz"* [The secret of a disguise], "Wax Flame" was subsequently republished with *"Las niñas desaparecidas"* [The girls who disappeared], a story which had appeared separately as a short novel in 1927. The final version of *Wax Flame*, published in 1931, incorporated a third tale, *"Cura de amor"* [Love's cure]. Notwithstanding the differences in date of publication and presumably of composition, all three stories represent a repudiation of simplistic divisions along national or moral lines.

In "Wax Flame," Concha Espina studies the traditional Spanish concept of honor in conjunction with the ancient debate on the advantages of city versus country life. With the opening paragraphs she describes the unexpected death of Rosaura, a young, robust mother of three who is married to Manuel, the master of a small railway station in the Santander region. Considerably older than his wife, Manuel had fought in the Spanish-American War and his contact with the exterior had both enlightened and disillusioned him. Illiterate prior to his military service, he was taught to read and write; but these skills brought with them a sensibility that caused him to reject the militaristic society he had initially admired. For Manuel, his return to his native Cantabria and his marriage to Rosaura represent a return to the pure, serene years of his youth. With Rosaura's death, he discovers that his identification of civilization with evil, rusticity with virtue is erroneous. He learns that José Luis, his young switchman and supposed friend, was actually his wife's lover and the father of her three sons.

A true son of nature, José Luis equates good with pleasure and love with physical gratification. He stands in marked contrast to the self-sacrificing Manuel, whose contacts with the "civilized" world have enabled him to overcome both primitive egotism and the false view of honor held by "civilized" society. Manuel rejects the traditional Spanish belief that the dishonor associated with marital infidelity falls as much on the husband and children of the adulterous woman as on the woman herself. Reasoning that the dishonor belongs to those who committed the infidelity, Manuel rejects the idea of vengeance and accepts the children as his own.

When the family goat senses Rosaura's absence and refuses to be milked, Manuel dresses himself in his dead wife's clothes in order to provide the children with milk. Equally indifferent to the derisive comments of the upper class train passengers who pull into the station at that moment and to José Luis' comment that no real man dresses in woman's clothing, Manuel symbolizes the incorporation of two conflicting systems. He is a product of both the "natural" and the "civilized" worlds; both contribute to his regeneration but neither traps him in the rigidity of its code.

Although repudiation of traditional attitudes towards honor appears repeatedly in contemporary Spanish literature, Concha Espina's handling of the theme is both novel and effective. For the reader, as for José Luis, Manuel's grotesque appearance brings a brief snicker of incredulity that gives way to a profound admiration as the full impact of the episode slowly transforms the comic surface meaning into a moving revelation of human benevolence.

"Love's Cure" contains a similar rejection of dialectical simplification. Once again, Concha Espina constructs the action around two erroneously paired couples: Gerardo Escobar and his wife Clara, and the North American Henry Dix and his Spanish fiancée Rosa. Originally engaged to Rosa, Gerardo inexplicably abandons her to marry the beautiful but insipid Clara. The couple has been married for less than a year when an automobile accident brings Rosa, her sister Emilia, and Dix to their home in search of help. Totally disenchanted with his wife, Gerardo promptly turns his attention to Rosa. Equally dissatisfied with her marriage, Clara aggressively pursues the wealthy and socially prominent Dix.

Capricious and egotistical, Clara glories in the prospect of entrapping—for the second time—a man already engaged to another woman. For her, a public scandal followed by a Reno-style divorce and then a life of luxury with Dix represent the twentieth-century ideal as imposed by North American culture. While Dix corroborates her vision of a morally corrupt United States with his stories of quick divorces followed by precipitous remarriages, he himself typifies more the constant lover of Hispanic tradition than the emotionally fickle individuals of his own description.

Initially presented as rather naive and superficial, Dix—like Manuel of "Wax Flame"—grows in stature during the course of the story. Genuinely in love with Rosa, he agrees to help Clara obtain her divorce and to marry her if this will enable Rosa to find happiness with Gerardo. For Rosa, the prospect of a reconciliation with her first and only real love is initially appealing. In the end, however she comes to realize that she can never forgive him for the suffering he has caused her and she abandons him to reconstruct her life with Dix. Her future is not, however, totally unclouded, for Gerardo's damage can never be fully undone. The memory of a love untainted by the experience of betrayal will continue to intrude on her relationship with Dix. Written in a natural, succinct style, "Love's Cure" is a simple narrative that subtly invalidates national stereotypes and at the same time points out the irreparable consequences of the sentimental frivolity fostered by contemporary society.

The insoluble conflict between contemporary society and traditional values also occupies a central position in "The Girls who

Disappeared." Based on a newspaper account of two runaways from a school for orphaned girls, the story investigates possible causes of an actual, historical event. After six years in the Madrid school, Ascensión Estrada has developed a cynical attitude toward the methods and motives of her teachers. She sees the school less as an educational facility than a cloister in which young girls are gradually brought into the religious order through indoctrination and isolation from the outside world. Narrated principally from Ascensión's perspective, the story does not pretend to capture objective truth. However, in this instance, what individuals perceive to be the truth is more important than what is objectively so.

Espina does not corroborate Ascensión's appraisal of the situation, but does strongly suggest that the seclusion of the students fosters a false view of reality that ultimately works against the religious and moral principles which the nuns endeavor to impart. For at least two of the younger nuns, the decision to enter the order was in fact based more on fear of life in the secular world than on a true religious calling. For both, life in the convent is an unhappy experience. Determined to avoid a similar fate, Ascensión agrees to elope with a military friend of her dead brother. Unaware that her fiancé's father has transferred his son to Andalucia in order to circumvent the elopement, Ascensión leaves the convent with another young girl equally ignorant of the world and similarly anxious to experience a fuller life. Only briefly deterred by the soldier's absence, Ascensión adamantly refuses to return to the convent. Totally unprepared to make their way in the world, the two girls proceed toward the center of Madrid where they are promptly lost in the crowd.

"The Girls who Disappeared" is neither an illustration of the principle that restraint inflames rebellion, as Smith contends,[3] nor is it a simple anecdote devoid of implications for religious education in general, as Felix García would have us believe.[4] Throughout the story, Concha Espina balances the negative and positive aspects of contemporary society and traditional values, refusing to align herself with either. In a society where two distinct value systems coexist in hostile opposition, there are two mutually exclusive explanations for every action. Thus, the term "disappeared" takes on a radically different meaning according to individual attitudes and perspectives.

For the Mother Superior and those committed to the preservation of innocence in a morally corrupt culture, it refers to the young runaways whose exposure to the outside world automatically precludes their return to the purity of the convent. For Ascensión and the proponents of modern society, the term signifies the involuntary seclusion of young girls in educational facilities that systematically repress their natural development. Equally critical of Spanish Catholicism for its inability to adapt to contemporary culture and of contemporary Spain for its failure to distinguish between a responsible exercise of liberty and unrestrained rejection of all traditional mores, Concha Espina simultaneously depicts the tragic consequences of the two extremes. On the one hand, she presents the frustrated maternalism of Sisters Amparo and Mercedes, two young girls who did disappear behind the convent walls; on the other, she suggests the inevitable prostitution of Ascensión and her friend, who disappear in the morally indifferent masses of contemporary Madrid. Written in a simple, at times journalistic style that appropriately conveys Concha Espina's distance from the conflicting values of the characters, "The Girls who Disappeared" is an excellent piece of literature. It is also a valuable social document that succinctly reflects the growing polarization of Spanish society in the decade preceding the Civil War.

IV   Concha Espina and the Feminist Novel

Although Espina's previous work deals with various problems confronting women in the modern world, it is not until 1929 that she publishes a fully "feminist" novel. In keeping with the theme of "The Girls who Disappeared", *La virgen prudente* [The prudent virgin] rejects both the traditional view of women and the external trappings of modern feminism in favor of a unique amalgam of past and present. The novel is not a simple treatise on the rights and responsibilities of modern women; rather, it is a study of contradictory tendencies, cultural pressures, and prejudices that condition women's attitudes. The novelist herself explains that the term "prudent virgin" is an ironical reference to the inverted values of the conventional Spanish woman.[6] Throughout the novel, Espina introduces a large cross section of the Spanish middle class, for whom honor, virtue, and religious sentiment are reduced to a meaningless social convention. The prime example of the type is ironically named Cándida Moraleja ("Candid Morals"), the protagonist's half-sister, whose sole aim in life is the preservation of an appearance of virtue in order to attract a suitable husband.

For both Cándida and her mother, Pura, religion is a purely social affair which enables them to mingle with others of similar background and disposition. Ignorant and proud of their ignorance, these women hide behind a superficial adherence to poorly-understood religious doctrine, condemning women who seek equality with men "and destroy their faith in pernicious books" (*OC*, I, 841). Concha Espina finds that this attitude prevails among Spanish women and that they are primarily to blame for the regressive attitudes towards women in Spain.

In contrast to her unscrupulous but outwardly virtuous contemporaries, symbolically named Aurora de España aspires to a genuine feminine intervention in public life. As she sees it, this would revolutionize the prevailing policies. Committed to the principles of justice and love for all human beings, Aurora pursues a career in law so that she might combat the vindictive legislation based on "an eye for an eye, a tooth for a tooth." Travel, native intelligence, a highly developed sensibility, and—perhaps most importantly—the absence of feminine influence in her early life contribute to Aurora's exceptional personality. Adopted by her paternal grandfather after her father's death, her education and ideals bear no relation to those of her half-sister or her mother. Whereas Cándida gleefully hypothesizes that her unborn sons will become army men, Aurora is deeply opposed to war and to the false patriotism that leads women to surrender their offspring to military causes.[6] Her attitude towards marriage is similarly at odds with the prevailing view. While her mother describes matrimony as a loveless experience that must be endured as the only social organism capable of resolving women's problems, Aurora envisions marriage as the absolute union of two individuals whose commitment to each other only intensifies their commitment to a commonly shared ideal.

A true example of independent thinking in her opposition to the death penalty, to the traditional concept of honor, and to the passive mediocrity of Spanish women, Aurora is nevertheless not fully emancipated from the romantic expectations for centuries associated with the feminine sex. Initially she gently rebuffs her suitors in the belief that a sentimental commitment will interfere with her plans. This attitude continues during her early days in Madrid, during which she tactfully discourages Guillermo Casal and Jaime Solinde, two purported candidates for Cándida's hand in marriage.

Aurora's defense of her doctoral thesis causes a minor uproar and leads her to the disillusioning discovery that her female colleagues neither sympathize with nor understand her ideas. This and the inevitable breaking off of relations with her mother and stepsister leave Aurora weakened and disheartened. Even those who seem genuinely receptive to her ideas and concerned for her welfare express skepticism as to the practicality of her goals. Guillermo Casal proposes that Aurora conceal her aspirations rather than squander her energies on those who cannot possibly comprehend her. Julia Rey, whose long-standing friendship and affection are indisputable, speaks of a need to clip Aurora's wings. Although Julia typifies the "emancipated" woman in her personal life, she is sufficiently influenced by the prevailing cultural norms to actively encourage Guillermo's interest in Aurora. She hopes that marriage will serve to moderate Aurora's activism and at the same time, to protect her from the intolerance of her antagonists.

Secretly torn between a need for security and a desire to chart a new path for herself, Aurora eventually succumbs to the gentle but persistent pressures of Guillermo and Julia. Characteristically, Aurora's sentimental commitment is absolute and, as Julia confesses with alarm, the risks are equally great. Convinced that love requires total trust, Aurora gradually surrenders her autonomy to Guillermo. Her error lies as much in her choice of lover as in her vision of love. Like many of Concha Espina's male characters, Guillermo slowly reveals traits that are consistent, given the advantages of hindsight, but not necessarily predictable. Simultaneously attracted and intimidated by Aurora's independence, he conceals his reservations until he feels assured that Aurora's destiny is irrevocably tied to his.

For Aurora, the belated discovery is not entirely unexpected although she has previously avoided any open confrontation, in part because her absolute commitment to Guillermo takes precedence over any hint of disagreement and in part because she is pregnant with Guillermo's child. Aurora tries with increasing difficulty to reconcile her image of Guillermo with his behavior. She silently observes his cruel treatment of Jaime Solinde and her stepfather, Severo Moraleja. She offers no verbal resistance when Guillermo advises her to abandon her studies for reasons of health and when he confesses that he would prefer that she subordinate her personal ambitions in order to further his own career. It is only when Guillermo blatantly presumes to have absolute control over her with his suggestion that marriage is less suitable to their relationship than an extramarital arrangement that Aurora awakens from her romantic stupor and unequivocally terminates their relationship.

In contrast to Cándida's friend Refugio and the other "prudent virgins" who prefer abortion to the public recognition of their dishonor, Aurora views her condition as the least reproachable of human "sins." She determines to confront the social opprobrium in such a way that her example will contribute to the abolition of female enslavement, in particular, to the unjust banishment of women and children whose only crime has been committed in the name of love. Having briefly succumbed to convention, Aurora resumes an independent course, accompanied this time by the previously rejected but ever-faithful Jaime Solinde.

According to Joaquín de Entrambasaguas, Aurora's surrender to Guillermo is inconsistent with her otherwise independent character.[7] Although in this period of her development, Aurora clearly departs from her initial course, the temporary loss of direction is understandable in the light of the cultural environment. With the exception of Jaime Solinde, no character fully supports her position and Jaime's support is undoubtedly influenced by his realization that her love presupposes a shared commitment. In the confrontation between authenticity and convention, virtually all uphold the latter in some form. Inevitably, Aurora herself succumbs in the hope that an acceptable balance can be reached but, as she subsequently learns, compromise signifies capitulation in a society where the scales are heavily weighted in favor of conventional behavior.

This unbalance is graphically represented in the distribution of characters: Aurora, as the sole proponent of authenticity, and on the other side, a multitude of minor characters who appear only long enough to establish their strict adherence to the established norms. Like many characters of Pérez Galdós, those of *The Prudent Virgin* vary in their idiosyncrasies but share an inordinate devotion to the status quo, be it religious, social or moral. In particular, Pura and Cándida attest to a Galdosian influence as does Severo Moraleja, whose resemblance to Ramón Villaamil of *Miau* is striking. Both men find themselves in unexpected opposition to the system that had previously governed their lives and both are forced to admit their ineptitude in the resulting conflict. Alternately pathetic and sublime, profound and deranged, Villaamil and Moraleja represent a healthy vein in an otherwise diseased body which ultimately proves too much for their feeble resistance. Both come to see life as less alluring than death and both seek liberation in suicide. Considerably less complex than Villaamil, Severo Moraleja is nevertheless an excellent study in human character. Like Manuel in "Wax Flame," he grows in stature in the course of the novel. The magnitude of his evolution provides a clear picture of the distance between Aurora's authenticity and the conventional behavior of her contemporaries.

According to Félix García and Rosenberg, *The Prudent Virgin* represents no real ideological change with respect to the preceding novels.[8] Although it is true that it does not mark a radical break with the past, there is a world of difference between this work and the novelist's earlier writing. Over the years, Concha Espina has moved from the exaltation of an essentially passive response to human injustice to the endorsement of active resistence. True to her early writing in that she continues to believe that suffering is an inevitable component of life, she now advocates a more aggressive commitment to the abolition of individual and collective injustice. The widening of horizons that can be observed during the preceding years continues in *The Prudent Virgin*. While it is not the most outstanding of her novels, neither does it mark the low point in her artistic career, as Gerardo Diego believes.[9] Except for occasional lapses into visionary rhetoric in the descriptions of Aurora and her ideals, the novel contains none of the weaknesses that appear in other novels. The characterization is solid, the style is extremely readable, and the content continues to be of interest. Atypical of her work in some respects, *The Prudent Virgin* is nevertheless essential to a full understanding of Espina's writings and at the same time, a valuable addition to her artistic production.

V *Stories from Around the World*

In 1930 Concha Espina published two collections of stories that reflect her travels in Europe and Latin America: *Copa de horizontes* [A cupful of horizons] and *Siete rayos de sol* [Seven sun rays]. *A Cupful of Horizons* contains stories of diverse geographical setting: Cuba, Russia, Mexico, and China, among others. Notwithstanding their geographical diversity, two themes provide a unifying framework for the individual narratives: the conviction that man is essentially the same throughout the world—as stated in the introduction to the collection—and the idea expressed in one of the stories that life frequently has an absurdly literary appearance. A number of stories address the question of human suffering in the uneventful course of ordinary life but, here Concha Espina affirms that the sentimental rapture that frequently precedes disillusionment is in itself ample reward. Also in contrast to her previous treatment of the theme, she often terminates the action with the vindication of the protagonist's cause. In "*Marcha nupcial*" ["Wedding march"] and "*Huerto de rosa*" ["Rose garden"] amorous betrayal is either averted or avenged while in "*El crimen de una sombra*" ["The crime of a shadow"], the ironies of fate work against the perpetrators of injustice. Although some of the stories convey a sense of arbitrary suffering, most suggest that destiny has a way of exacting restitution.

For the most part, the remaining stories draw from historical events or anecdotes that attract Concha Espina's attention because of their "fictional" quality. The unlikely adventurer who ends his days as a general in China and the Russian pacifist drafted into the Spanish army have the appearance of being "literary" creations but are actually factual in origin. When compared with Concha Espina's earlier collections of short stories and in keeping with the style of the immediately preceding works, *A Cupful of Horizons* is written in a relatively unadorned prose that is fluid and refreshing. In terms of the content, however, the stories are often unduly complicated by references to past events not pertinent to the action.

By Concha Espina's own testimony, *Seven Sun Rays* proposes to do for Spain what the Grimm brothers did for Germany. The stories are artistic renditions of folk tales previously collected by Aurelio Espinosa in Spain and Latin America. With her belief in the importance of tradition, Concha Espina saw the oral preservation of ancient folklore as a sign of cultural continuity in the Spanish-speaking world. Her reworking of the popular material in a more literary form undoubtedly has as its aim the propagation of the traditional spirit to those classes increasingly less rooted in their heritage. Though she originally intended to publish several volumes of a similar nature, various other projects and the outbreak of the Spanish Civil War prevented her completing the collection.

Closer to the "fairy tale" than to the earthy, often ribald folk tales of many collections, the stories in *Seven Sun Rays* offer a deliberately stylized view of reality with a predominance of religious and moralistic themes. In virtually all of them, good triumphs over evil and fantasy prevails over verisimilitude. Perfectly executed both in style and in the organization of materials, the stories cannot compete with the delightfully unpolished products of popular literature on which they are based. Like much "cultured" art, they lose in spontaneity what they gain in artistic perfection.

VI   *Travel Impressions and Political Ideology*

It is not until 1932, four years after her visit to the Caribbean islands and the United States that Espina publishes her impressions in *Singladuras* [Day's run]. The book is interesting as a reflection of the novelist's attitudes during this period, offering a clearer picture of her personal values than a novel, where authorial views are often shaded by the psychological requirements of characterization. Furthermore, exposure to a new culture forces her to define more fully her own beliefs. While this applies to her travels to Germany, it is all the more noticeable with respect to the creole and "yankee" cultures.

In *Day's Run* Concha Espina strongly states her opposition to the dictatorial regime of Gerardo Machado in Cuba and to United States imperialism in Puerto Rico. Her reaction to racism in both Cuba and the United States is equally strong and although she speaks of the black race with slightly patronizing tones, she clearly advocates their full integration into society. Espina's interest in the Sephardic Jews continues and she observes their marginal assimilation in the United States with disgust. In general, her views would appear to coincide with those of the conservative left. She clearly sees a need for change but consistently repudiates violence as a vehicle for social transformation. Holding Ghandi in high esteem, she writes approvingly of pacifism in general.

Written in the final years of Primo de Rivera's dictatorship in Spain, *Day's Run* gives little evidence of the radical split soon to break Spanish society into two hostile camps. In New York, Concha Espina feels very much at home in the company of Federico García Lorca, León Felipe, and others subsequently identified with the Republican government that she will oppose. However, there are signs that she was not totally comfortable with certain changes then beginning to appear. Like many Spaniards, Concha Espina considers herself an individualist—and as such, is strongly averse to mass movements. Therefore, she refused to join women's groups although she reiterates her support for feminist activities. Her endorsement of all movements of liberation is tempered by a moralistic tendency that never disappears from her work. In her speech before a women's group in Cuba, she prefers to stress their responsibilities over their rights.[10] At this time, she advocates an uneasy balance of the two in all areas of social change. With time, the equilibrium shifts so that responsibility, often implying self-restraint, takes precedence over rights.

The inconsistencies that underlie her thinking can be seen in her attitude towards working students at Middlebury College. On the one hand, Espina is proud of the financial independence secured through her own labor. At the same time, she is somewhat disdainful of those students who wait on tables in the college dining hall in return for free tuition. She confesses that she could never bring herself to serve tables for any amount of money and she finds the students' expectation of a tip indicative of their lack of dignity. Notwithstanding her advocacy of an "aristocracy of talent," based on individual merit rather than inherited privilege, she is unable to throw off the values of her upbringing and continues to equate an individual's work with his social status.

The influence of her early education is similarly visible in her attitude towards the Protestant sects, which she describes as "discredited, vacillating, with neither inspiration nor warmth, but boiling like any other fashion or novelty. . . . a collection of names in which the soul is dispersed, far from that which is a noble view of the immutable and eternal."[11] Less concerned with dogma than the ceremonial differences between her Catholicism and the varieties of Protestantism that she observes, Concha Espina's repudiation of the latter reveals an intransigence strengthened in the coming years. It should be noted, however, that in general *Day's Run* contains little of the intolerance brought on by the Civil War. Like *Seeds*, it is written in an extremely simple, nonrhetorical language that communicates a sense of ideological moderation. For the most part, Concha Espina continues to demonstrate an openness to change and on occasion, an active advocacy of social transformation.

CHAPTER 7

The Spanish Republic and the Civil War Years

I *The* Folletín *and the Beginnings of Political Partisanship*

CONCHA Espina's next novel initiates a series of highly politicized works that are of interest only from a sociological or historical point of view. Artistically, they represent the lowest point in her literary career, combining the weaknesses of her previous writing with the rhetoric and partisan vision of political propaganda. The shift is not immediately evident in *Flor de ayer* [Yesterday's flower] where it appears that Concha Espina originally intended to write another sentimental novel with no specific references to contemporary politics.

Closer to the *folletín* in the early chapters than to the political novel, *Yesterday's Flower* opens with the dramatic introduction of the protagonist, Victoria García, who is heard crying outside the Cantabrian manor of her father, Antonio Quintaval. Victoria's mother is a country woman who was seduced and later abandoned by Antonio. Now nine years old, Victoria has been rejected by her father and only moderately attended to by her mother. Although Engracia, Antonio's sister, would like to adopt the child, Antonio threatens to reveal her love letters to Armando Lecuna, written after her marriage to Ramón Zárate. Antonio's insinuation of Engracia's adultery is false but Engracia fears to have the matter publicized.

From this point on the plot becomes increasingly complicated. The reader is gradually informed that Lecuna was killed by Antonio at Ramón's command. The villainous Ramón continues to persecute his wife and Victoria throughout the novel. When Engracia persists in raising her niece, it is Ramón who pays the impoverished Antonio to invoke his paternal rights and intern Victoria in a school in Madrid. Although Engracia continues to visit Victoria and in fact pays for her schooling, she feels powerless to protect her. Engracia's unwillingness to stand up to Antonio is but one of several elements in the novel that is not adequately explained. She watches helplessly when Victoria is removed from the school at sixteen and put to work as her father's housekeeper. Now addicted to morphine, Antonio watches indifferently Ramón's attempts to pervert the girl. When Ramón is unable to overcome Victoria's hatred for him, he incites his son Esteban to seduce her, playing on Esteban's interest in the girl and his jealousy of Lorenzo Alcaín, whom Victoria had met briefly as a child and again during her final months in the boarding school.

Although Concha Espina describes Lorenzo as the male equivalent to her exquisitely sensitive heroines, his conduct hardly matches this description. Despite his romantic interest in Victoria, he falls deeply in love with Engracia and it is only at her request that he persists in his efforts to help Victoria. Furthermore, Lorenzo inexplicably conceals his marriage to another woman until his wife appears unannounced and leaves their four-year-old daughter with the dumbfounded Victoria. The inconsistent characterization of Lorenzo, Engracia, and others, in addition to the absurd complications of plot, rob the novel of value. In part the changing nature of the characters stems from Concha Espina's shift in political attitudes. Towards the middle of the novel, allusions to contemporary politics become more and more frequent. The occasional criticism of contemporary Spanish culture gives way to a radical repudiation of the Republican government and an unrestrained endorsement of the Falangist movement.

Esteban, Ramón's former partner in the campaign to pervert Victoria, resurfaces as a dedicated propagandist for the Falange who dies at the hands of the Communists while trying to disseminate his party's literature. Coincidentally, his political conversion accompanies a moral regeneration. Initially Lorenzo is portrayed as a sincere Communist and although Concha Espina continues to use this label in referring to him, his political beliefs undergo a radical change in the course of the novel. His exaltation of traditional Hispanic values, his elitist view of human nature and his extremely religious spirit as revealed in the latter part of the novel coincide with Falangist party literature in both terminology and content.

Victoria also becomes a spokesperson for Falangist ideology in the second half of the book. She dreams of leading Madrid's lower classes back to the rural communities of their ancestors where they can reestablish their true roots. She reaches the conclusion that the Spanish people require a strong chief or commander to lead them to new forms of life based on traditional Spanish values. Pursuing these values, Victoria severs her relationship with Lorenzo until he is legally free to join her. After a brief visit to her Cantabrian birthplace, she leaves for America in what she conceives as a journey in search of the old values.

Characteristically, Concha Espina expresses her ideas with an imprecision that hinders real understanding. While she is clearly partisan to the Falangist movement, it is difficult to ascertain the specific items in their program that elicit her support. Founded in 1933 but active under different names in the preceding years, the Falangist Party undergoes a series of ideological changes so that any attempt to reconstruct Concha Espina's ideas on the basis of party platform is of questionable value. Judging by *Yesterday's Flower*, it can be said that she advocates a national renaissance grounded in Spain's moral and spiritual heritage. She continues to speak favorably of pacifism and one of the characters with whom she agrees in other aspects decries the militaristic spirit that is so characteristic of Spanish society (*OC*, I, 1002).

Unlike the Nazi movement, Spanish Fascism has no antisemitic or racial overtones and Concha Espina explicitly repudiates this aspect of European Fascism. Falangism is, however, intensely nationalistic and this element is clearly visible in *Yesterday's Flower*. Neither this nor the exaltation of traditional values is new in Concha Espina but here it is accompanied by a rejection of modern society whereas formerly, emphasis fell on a fusion of the old and the new. Glen Parks, Lorenzo's half-Cuban and half-North American wife, represents the emotional superficiality and moral indifference that is presented as characteristic of modern society. Constantly in pursuit of new pleasures, Glen is incapable of love in the pure, selfless sense that Concha Espina defines it. She casually enters into marriage and just as casually rids herself of her husband and their child. Like the morphine-addicted Antonio and the sexually aberrant Ramón, Glen is a product of the contemporary culture slowly undermining Spain's true character.

Once again, Concha Espina's desire to contrast two opposing systems causes her to exaggerate their respective evils and virtues. In *Yesterday's Flower* and in the novels that follow, this tendency is intensified by the political sectarianism of the period. These works not only offer a partisan representation of reality, they often adjust the facts to fit the desired view. Characters become representatives of a particular set of beliefs, dialogue disappears and the discussion of values or ideologies predominates. This is only partially true of *Yesterday's Flower*, as the early part of the novel is generally devoid of political commentary. Unfortunately, the early chapters also suffer from a distorted view of reality which has its origins in the *folletín* and is equally subversive in terms of literary quality.

II   *Traditionalism and a New Look at Women's Aspirations*

Candelabro [Candelabra], like *Yesterday's Flower*, is published in 1933 but at least one of the stories included in the volume dates back to 1919 when it appeared in *The Prince of Song*. Although the other stories are not dated, all reflect the nationalistic spirit and the exaltation of traditional values that culminates during this period of Concha Espina's work. In *"Arboladuras"* ["Masts"], Jacinto is the oldest son of a rural family almost religious in its devotion to the traditions and legends of its past. He abruptly abandons both his childhood sweetheart and his life-long ambition to be a shepherd, as were his forefathers, to marry the daughter of a fisherman. Equally encomiastic of the seafaring and pastoral branches of Cantabrian society, Concha Espina clearly suggests that the break with tradition cannot be made without a loss of personal direction and con-sequently, individual happiness. In what can easily be construed as a parable of modern Spain, Jacinto repudiates his heritage to embrace a foreign life style with different values and symbols only to discover that his sense of purpose is irrevocably tied to the past that he has rejected. The initial allure of these novel forms of life soon wears off and Jacinto sadly realizes that he has lost all that gives meaning to his life. Unable to return to the mountains, he offers no resistance when his fishing boat sinks in a coastal storm, preferring death to the senseless existence that he erroneously chose.

In "Masts" and other stories in the volume, the characters' individuality is subordinated to symbolic value. Reflections of racial or regional characteristics, they are either stereotypes or archetypes who quickly fade from the reader's memory. Although there is some of this in "Blanca Uría," the ambiguous ending prevents the story from becoming yet another ideological statement. The evident shift to the right does not completely predetermine the outcome of the story or the characterization.

"Blanca Uría" recounts the unlikely case of Blanca, an illegitimate concert pianist who receives a marriage proposal from the man who was once married to her deceased mother. In some respects, it is a reworking of *The Prudent Virgin* along traditional lines. Despite her apparent self-sufficiency, professional success, and resulting prosperity, Blanca's only real desire in life is to attain the emotional fulfillment as wife and mother that her own mother casually squandered. Torn between her impulse for domestic security and her moral obligation to reveal the nature of their relationship to her suitor, Blanca opts for the second course of action. Although the opportunity for a reconciliation remains open, the final paragraphs suggest that her moral victory closes the door to a possible marriage. Notwithstanding the improbable circumstances and somewhat rigid characterization, "Blanca Uría" surpasses the other stories in *Candelabra*, largely because Blanca's conflict cannot be reduced to a moralistic formula. The situation is ambiguous and the response to it is of necessity equivocal. Unlike most of Concha Espina's literature during this period, "Blanca Uría" analyzes the blurred zones of moral responsibility that constitute the greater part of human experience.

III   *The Poetic Expression of Sentimental Tragedy*

Although Concha Espina continues to write poetry throughout her life, it is not until 1933 that she publishes her second volume of poems. *Entre la noche y el mar* [Between the night and the sea] contains thirty compositions written between 1915 and 1933. In form, the poems vary greatly, ranging from the classical sonnet to the traditional *romance*.[1] Lexically, the book reflects a desire to "rehabilitate Spanish words that have been forgotten for Gallicisms or neologisms."[2] Throughout her career, Espina is constantly enriching her vocabulary in order to purify and at the same time expand the Spanish language.

In contrast to *My Flowers*, *Between the Night and the Sea* contains little of the sentimental introspection that characterizes her early writing. A number of the poems are inspired by her travels or are dedicated to friends and family members. Carefully constructed with respect to form, these poems are otherwise of limited interest. While in the novel, Concha Espina excels when she goes beyond the limits of her own sentimental experience, in her poetry the reverse is true. Among the many rather dry compositions in *Between the Night and the Sea*, the reader suddenly comes upon one or two poems that reveal the writer's suffering in a way that her prose can never convey it. In particular, *"Insomnio"* ["Insomnia"] and *"Delante de mi estatua"* ["Before my statue"] communicate a very real sense of lost happiness and her struggle to overcome a destiny that was not of her choosing.

IV *The Civil War from Behind the Lines*

Between 1933 and 1939, the upheaval preceding the Spanish Civil War and the war itself prevented Espina from publishing. According to a note added to *Moneda blanca* [White coin], three works initiated before 1936 were destroyed by the Republican forces occupying Luzmela until August of 1937. Of the works saved from destruction, *Retaguardia* was the first to be published, being printed in Nationalist-held territory a full year and a half before the war ends. Written during Concha Espina's months of house arrest, *Retaguardia* is contemporaneous with the events narrated. In this respect, it differs from much Civil War literature, composed after the conflict ended because most authors were actively fighting in the war. Unable to intervene in any meaningful way, Concha Espina naturally turned to writing as her only vehicle for active participation.

Subtitled "A Strictly Historical Novel in its Most Outstanding Episodes," *Retaguardia* takes place in Torremar—the novelist's fictional name for Santander—prior to its liberation by the Nationalist Army. The story opens with the disclosure that Alicia Quiroga's fiancé Rafael has disappeared. Although Alicia's family is prominent in local Republican politics, both she and her brother have come to repudiate their parents' views, largely under the influence of Rafael Ortiz and his sister Rosa. The Ortiz as well as the Quiroga family are members of Torremar's upper middle class. However, the Quirogas have only recently risen to their present status, while the Ortiz family comes from old *hidalgo* stock.

In Concha Espina's view, the divergent backgrounds give rise to distinct values that can be seen in both the moral conduct and the political loyalties of the family members. Citing Vicente Espinel, she observes that "There are two classes of favored individuals; those who rose from humble beginnings to gain the leader's grace, and these want everything for themselves. Others, noble lords in origin who have been received and loved by their king; these, since they were born princes, want to share their well-being with everyone."[3] Concha Espina applies this classification of human conduct to contemporary Spanish society in *Retaguardia*, equating materialistic self-interest with the newly wealthy and dedication to the nation's welfare with the long-established bourgeoisie.

For Antonio and Manuela Quiroga, the advent of the Republic and the outbreak of war offer a unique opportunity to accelerate their climb up the social and economic ladder. In spite of the shortage of food in Torremar, they are able to maintain a very comfortable life style through their influence and the black market. They pay lip service to Communism but make no sacrifices to further the Republican war effort.[4] By contrast, the Ortiz family has lost most of its moderate wealth as a result of conservative politics. With one son imprisoned on the *Satan*—a ship where purported Nationalist sympathizers are held—and another who crossed enemy lines to join Franco's forces, Rafael's disappearance leaves only Rosa to support her parents both emotionally and financially.

The rest of the novel recounts the unsuccessful efforts of Alicia, her brother Felipe, and Rosa to locate Rafael. Although many incidents in *Retaguardia* are based on actual events, the novelist's pretension of historical accuracy is illusory. History must take into account the conflicting, often paradoxical elements that move individuals to react in a given set of circumstances. Concha Espina sees no paradoxes; unlike the historian, she does not proceed from data to analysis but from personal conviction to interpretation of events. In *Retaguardia*, the forces of good—the Nationalists—oppose the forces of evil—the Republicans. Despite Concha Espina's assertion that the division does not coincide with social hierarchy (*OC*, I, 1023), she obviously perceives the conflict in terms of social classes. According to her personal estimation, Falangist support comes from artists, doctors, university graduates, the diplomatic corps and the aristocracy while the Republicans count among their ranks barbers, shopboys, factory workers, waiters and "various types of illiterates and loafers; those devoid of merits and values, the people of low life, the spiteful and envious ones" (*OC*, I, 1051).

Throughout *Retaguardia*, these same criteria govern the presentation of characters. Although on two occasions Concha Espina suggests that the lower classes are perhaps merely ignorant tools of their leaders (also of humble origins), in general she emphasizes their brutality more than their ignorance. Only in her presentation of Vicente, a professional deep-sea diver whom Alicia enlists in her efforts to locate Rafael, is there any deviation from the pattern and in this case, travel, education, and Alicia's ennobling influence set him apart from his class of origin. Furthermore, as a member of a seafaring caste, Vicente considers himself superior and distinct from his nonmaritime social counterparts.

There is clearly some truth in Concha Espina's portrayal of Nationalist heroism and Communist depravity but her categorical identification of the left with evil and the right with good is excessive. Although it is perhaps unreasonable to expect objectivity in the Civil War novelists, a novel that does not even attempt to comprehend the conflict lacks literary and historical value. Ironically, Concha Espina's assertion that political rhetoric and ideological preconceptions dominate the leftist press (*OC*, I, 1042 and 1057) is equally true of her own book.

Retaguardia must be read as a reflection of the passions that dismembered Spain during the Civil War. When a basically gentle, compassionate individual yields to the intransigence that swept the country, the violence and hatred that characterize both the right and the left become somewhat more comprehensible. For Concha Espina, as for the great majority of Spaniards, the need to justify the rightness of their cause leads to a disjointed set of values. In *Retaguardia,* the fact that the conservative, upper-class women are forced to do manual labor two days a week for five-hour shifts or that the rose gardens have been destroyed to plant vegetables is viewed with outrage. This, however, would not be objectionable if the novelist did not excuse the Nationalist bombing of civilian targets, blaming the casualties on the irresponsible Republican authorities who fail to maintain an adequate air raid system.

Stylistically, political rhetoric supercedes artistic expression in all but two episodes in *Retaguardia:* Felipe's visit to the *Satan* and Vicente's descent into the Bay of Biscay. There is a definite political slant in the novelist's description of the cold-blooded executions on the *Satan.* However, there is a disturbing ring of truth in her depiction of the Republican executioners who have become so habituated to violence that killing has become a tedious, fatiguing activity. The nightmare of war comes across even more forcefully in the description of Vicente's dive. Bound by his promise to help Alicia find Rafael, Vicente descends into the coastal waters that serve as a mass burial ground for Nationalist sympathizers, only to find himself in a world that has all the disquieting qualities of a surrealistic dream: "A multitude of men raised to an upright position by the force of the water, anchored in the mire by the lead that was tied to their feet, bitten by the crabs and other fish, saturated with brackish sorrow, rigid in their positions of terror, they waver awfully" (*OC*, I, 1067). With each change of the current, the floating bodies recede or advance. They seem to beckon to Vicente with their hands or move towards him in a collective dance. At one point a single body is propelled by the current and rushes at Vicente who notes with horror that the dead man's lips are sewn shut with safety pins. Historical or invented, the description of the underground graveyard is a literary *tour de force* of incredible impact. In contrast to the bulk of the novel, in this episode hackneyed rhetoric does not subvert literary effect.

V *The Civil War and the Literature of Political Partisanship*

Written in 1938, *Luna roja* [Red moon] is a collection of stories about the Civil War. The prologue again echoes the politically motivated identification of evil with the left and good with the right observed in *Retaguardia*. The war is here described as a battle between material and spirit, darkness and light, Satan and God. While many stories are constructed along these lines, at least one appears to have been written before the war, prior to the novelist's total break with the Republican government. *"El Dios de los niños"* ["The childrens' God"] describes the miners' uprising in Oviedo during October of 1934, some twenty-one months before the military hostilities. The novelist upholds the justice of the miners' demands but condemns their blind submission to a handful of Communist agitators whose only aim is destruction and a new form of enslavement.

As a contrast to the misguided miners, Concha Espina creates the figure of Xuanuco, a small farmer who represents traditional Asturian values of justice, compassion, and veneration for women. The uprising surprises Xuanuco during a visit to Oviedo and forces him to take shelter in a private home with a number of other citizens. There he meets two women who are on their way to get their children at the School for Christian Doctrine. Forced to abandon the house when angry miners set it on fire, Xuanuco, Julia, and Marta learn that the school has also been set on fire. Although all the children miraculously escape from the burning building, Julia is wounded before reaching her two sons and taken to a makeshift hospital. Moved by a sense of Christian obligation and deeply interested in the young, attractive widow, Xuanuco places the children in the care of neighbors, manages to locate their mother, and proposes to return with them to the Asturian countryside. The purifying effect of rural life, first suggested as a solution to Spain's political disorder in *Yesterday's Flower*, reappears in "The Children's God" in conjunction with the presentation of the Nationalist cause as divinely protected. Although the rest of the stories in *Red Moon* maintain the religious interpretation of the war, the exaltation of rural Spain and its inhabitants disappears.

The characters in *"Tragedia rural"* ["Rural tragedy"] are drawn from the Spanish upper class. Typically, they are portrayed as intrinsically superior in sensibility and moral stature. Autobiographical in a number of its details, the story relates the experiences of Dolores Valdor and her four-year-old daughter Paloma during the Communist control of Luzmela. Subjected to frequent searches and cut off from her friends and her husband, who has been jailed as a Nationalist sympathizer, Dolores struggles to provide her daughter with some semblance of a normal childhood.

Paloma's only diversions are a doll that cries and her pet lamb, Lucero. During one of the searches, a Communist official cuts the doll open, believing that the mechanism that makes it cry is a hiding place for secret documents. Evincing what is identified as innate individualism, Paloma violently rejects the mended doll that now neither cries nor blinks its eyes. Her illusion has been shattered and she will not admit a mediocre substitute. Turning her attention to Lucero, Paloma faces yet another disillusionment when a wolf enters the lamb's shelter. Innocently, Paloma offers the wolf a piece of her bread and protests when the terror stricken family maid removes her to the house. In defiance of natural law, the wolf does not eat the lamb; the next day, he is found dead of starvation next to the open door of the lamb's shelter.

In *"El hombre y el mastín"* ["The man and the mastiff"], the religious sentimentalism of "Rural Tragedy" yields to a more substantial discussion of the ideological conflict underlying the military confrontation. Characteristically, the Communists are depicted as uneducated, morally insidious individuals who seek to annihilate the social hierarchy because they are basically inferior and know they cannot improve their position in any other manner. Easily duped by Communist propaganda, the ignorant peasants of Luzmela rapidly abandon their traditions in favor of free love, modern dress, and the rhetoric of social equality. In particular, the protagonist's fiancé undergoes a radical change in character that culminates in his attempt to rape the young girl. As in "Rural Tragedy" animals are shown to be less brutal than their human counterparts; the would-be victim is saved by her dog, who kills the assailant with a single neck bite.

The plot of "The Man and the Mastiff" is considerably less interesting than the reconstructed political debate between a Communist propagandist and don Luis, a local doctor. Clearly speaking for the novelist, the doctor provides a detailed view of Concha Espina's political ideology during this period. According to don Luis, religious faith takes precedence over all human rights. Furthermore, because the social hierarcy is divinely ordained, it is incorrect to question the wisdom of providence which is superior to any human design. Violently opposed to the "discredited demand for equality" (*OC*, II, 613), he maintains that those who have acquired privilege through merit and those who have received privilege at birth (and utilized it responsibly) cannot be faulted. Not entirely committed to the *status quo*, don Luis advocates a return to the medieval situation, when each individual could (allegedly) forge his own destiny and create his fortune on the basis of merit. Somewhat vague in his proposals for a medieval renaissance, don Luis terminates his speech with a confession of his Falangism and the statement that the government will belong to the people when they improve themselves.

The proof that don Luis' ideas correspond to those of Concha Espina and represent a break with her prewar attitudes can be found in *"La carpeta gris"* ["The gray file"]. Autobiographical in nearly every detail, the story describes the incident in which Concha Espina's granddaughter is forced to dispose of an incriminating manuscript during a Communist search of their home in Luzmela. Thoroughly disillusioned with the Spain that she has previously exalted in her literature, Concha Espina composes "The Gray File" to substantiate her contention that the Spanish lower class has proven itself unworthy of her trust. The local children, whom she has clothed and fed, repay her generosity by uprooting her garden and verbally abusing her. The gardener whom she has employed for many years reports her literary activity to the local government and the two Communist refugees placed in her home abuse her hospitality. For Concha Espina, these incidents are proof that her novelistic representation of the Spanish lower class is absurdly out of touch with reality.

Like don Luis in "The Man and the Mastiff," she now believes that "there are no rights outside the law of God" (*OC*, II, 629) and that only a select minority can ever hope to attain the moral excellence that she once viewed as an intrinsic aspect of national character. The absolute faith in the correctness of her position leads to an uncharacteristically smug self-portrait. Generally modest in her appraisal of her own merits, Concha Espina here holds herself up as a model of superior, natively aristocratic deportment who gains the envious respect of her vulgar houseguests and the unwavering love of a rejected suitor. The selfrighteousness that accompanies political intransigence gradually injects itself into Concha Espina's self-image. Fortunately, in this and in other respects, the change is short lived.

VI   *Concha Espina's Autobiographical Account of the War*

Esclavitud y Libertad—Diario de una prisionera [Slavery and liberty—diary of a prisoner] is an autobiographical account of Concha Espina's war experiences. Much of the information included in the diary had already appeared as fiction; the only real differences lie in the identification of individuals by their real names and the adoption of a slightly less rhetorical language. Again, it should be pointed out that Concha Espina tends to express herself more naturally in her nonfictional writing, although in this work the political slant makes the change less noticeable.

Slavery and Liberty naturally reveals more about Espina's sources of information than the preceding works and this is of importance in understanding her view of the conflict. She dismisses the local press reports as Republican propaganda, but her own information is no more reliable. Although insisting that her facts are accurate because they come from foreign newspapers, she simultaneously reveals that her sources are German, of dubious veracity. Furthermore, her access to German newspapers was limited and without a radio—an invention she personally disliked at this point in her life—she was unable to receive Nationalist broadcasts. Consequently, the bulk of her information comes from friends who frequently have only a secondhand knowledge of the actual events. The episode in *Retaguardia* in which Rosa is forced to scrub floors is based on a report from Concha Espina's cousins of this occurrence in other localities.

The extent to which the writer relies on the Nationalist interpretation of events and her absolute faith in its veracity can be seen in her discussion of the destruction of Guernica. It is generally known that this ancient city was leveled by German planes in an unprecedented bombing of civilian targets that was later to be a common German practice during World War II. According to Concha Espina, the Basque town was destroyed by Russians in a perverse attempt to prevent it from falling into enemy hands. Once again, Espina exemplifies the tragic consequences of the Spanish Civil War during which truth became an instrument of political expediency and individuals who normally might be expected to respond very differently, blindly accept the dictates of their respective parties.

VII   *Reworking of a Sentimental Story in the Light of the War*

Concha Espina's next work is the most politically dictated of her Civil War publications. Written during the latter part of the war, *Las alas invencibles* [Invincible wings] represents a shift from the exaltation of Falangist ideology to the glorification of Franco and the military. Again, Concha Espina serves as a barometer for the political attitudes of a large segment of the nation which gradually adopted Franco's rhetoric of national defense after the death of José Antonio, founder of the Falangist Party. The first chapter of the novel is a republication of "Wild Canary," the short story originally published in *Ivory Distaffs*. In the novelistic version, the aviator with whom Talín falls in love is renamed Fidel and the original ending is totally transformed. In both versions, the action terminates with an airplane ride, but in the original story the flight enables personal fulfillment through voluntary death while in the novel, Talín's journey leads to a new life in Nationalist Spain.

In *Invincible Wings* Talín comes to symbolize the Spanish nation and the triumph of the traditional ruling class over the lower class. Both Fidel, the aviator from a socially prominent family, and Pedro, a Communist laborer who subsequently espouses the Nationalist cause, are in love with Talín but in the end, Pedro cordially relinquishes his claim. It is Pedro who carries Talín to the hanger where Fidel is warming the plane for takeoff. The rhetoric of the preceding novels seems moderate in comparison to the language employed in *Invincible Wings*. The Communists are now described as coconspirators with Stalin in a plan to establish a Russian border on the Atlantic. The emphasis on Falangist resistance shifts to a glorification of military aggresion in which the rights of conquest are upheld as the final arbiter of social organization. José Antonio's name is replaced by that of Francisco Franco who leads his "retinue of remarkable generals" and the "bravest soldiers in the world" to a divinely ordained victory in the "most admirable war in the universe."[5] It is a sad commentary on the period that a woman who once advocated pacifism should come to exalt war in this manner. With *Invincible Wings*, political rhetoric totally excludes artistic value.

VIII   *Religion and Politics in the Interpretation of History*

Although some of the rhetoric observed in *Invincible Wings*
appears in *Princesas del martirio* [Martyred princesses], the emphasis
is more on the religious than the political character of the Nationalist
movement. Furthermore, the case of three Red Cross nurses mur-
dered by Republican soldiers is based on the judicial investigation of
the incident and the language of legal testimony which emerges at
various moments in the story establishes a somewhat more "objective" tone. Concha Espina compares the nurses' deaths to the
martyrdom of Christ and the early Christians. Thus, the drawing of
lots for the nurses' clothing echoes Christ's death. Similarly, the
tortuous walk towards an "unknown Calvary" and the nurses' being
killed at three o'clock in the afternoon reiterate the parallel with the
Crucifixion. The fusion of religion and politics can be seen in the
description of a Nationalist plane, with its wings opened in the sign of
the cross, and the portrayal of the dying nurses, who are tied with two
Nationalist soldiers to form the Fascist symbol of the yoke and the five
arrows.

Constant allusions to the historical, political, and religious
significance of the events lessen the story's impact. The military
attack on a medical facility, the murder of wounded soldiers housed in
the hospital, the burning to death of the doctor, and the rape and
execution of the nurses speak for themselves. The repeated references to Communist brutality and the juxtaposition of political-
religious symbols are both unnecessary and counterproductive. The
undeniable horror of the episode is lost in subjective commentary
that prompts the reader to dismiss the account as pure propaganda.

CHAPTER 8

Literature During the PostWar Period

I *The Rhetoric of National Exultation*

WITH the end of the war, the painstaking process of national reconstruction begins. Even without the imposition of government censorship, the desire of those remaining in Spain to reassume some order would probably have prevented substantive discussions of the contemporary socio-political reality. Between 1939 and the late 1940's, writers in Spain purposely sidestep most issues confronting the nation since the acknowledgment of conflict would suggest that Franco's victory was not, in fact, the answer to the country's problems. Naturally, much literature during this period deals with the war experience, but little effort is made to study the causes or the effects of the conflict. Unlike the Republican exiles who are forced by their defeat to seek an explanation for their loss and to rebuild their lives in alien cultures, the Nationalists can look to their military victory as proof of the validity of their cause. The rhetoric of the war years disappears very gradually and meanwhile literature becomes a vehicle for national exultation.

Concha Espina's biography of Saint Casilda exemplifies the tendency to select subject matter that appropriately reflects the values of postwar Spanish society. Born in the eleventh century, Casilda was a Moorish princess who converted to Catholicism. She provides an early example of the religious fervor that Concha Espina attributes to the national character. Modern Spain is seen herein as a continuation of the medieval period. In both periods, Espina represents Christian ideals in a world threatened by pagan invaders. The description of Moorish Spain also serves to justify the use of Moroccan legionaires in the Nationalist war effort for, as Concha Espina repeatedly points out in her biography, the Moors are an integral part of Spanish ancestry. Alternately objective in its reliance on biographical data, and subjective in its interpretation of national character, *Casilda of Toledo* is intrinsically of little interest. Nevertheless, it represents Concha Espina's first postwar attempt to put aside the conflict and derive her literary inspiration from other sources. Unable for the present to transcend the rhetoric of Nationalist exultation, with time she will reestablish greater artistic autonomy.

II *Postwar Conformity and a Return to Drama*

The desire to leave the Civil War behind is evident in Concha Espina's first dramatic work since 1918 *(The Foundling)*. To a large degree, the sentimental conflict in *La tiniebla encendida* [Enlightened darkness] recalls that of *To Wake up and Die*. In both works, the protagonists are sensitive individuals married to beautiful but coldly egotistical women. Both discover belatedly that they have permanently cut themselves off from the one woman who could truly share their aspirations. Whereas Diego's relationahip with Pilar in *To Wake Up and Die* does not develop until after their respective marriages, Ignacio is originally engaged to Mercedes and voluntarily retracts his promise in order to marry Flora. In both the play and the earlier novel, Concha Espina contrasts the noble values of the central characters with the insipid, morally deficient norms of contemporary society.

The criticism in *Enlightened Darkness* is, however, considerably more moderate than in *To Wake Up and Die* and the number of individuals corrupted by modern society is smaller. In the postwar atmosphere, the tendency to sidestep conflict necessarily debilitates the portrayal of problematic human relationships. The antagonists in the play remain on the periphery of the action, with only a marginal connection to Ignacio's internal struggle. Pedro Gómez, the ambitious but incompetent journalist who feigns a romantic interest in Ignacio's sister and in Flora so that he can borrow Ignacio's signature for his own poorly written articles has no function in the play other than to underscore Ignacio's superiority. The same can be said for Camilo and Pepita Infanta who appear briefly as representatives of a superficial social set that Ignacio and his family tolerate only out of courtesy. Pedro's portrait, as well as those of the Infantas is an amusing caricature of certain human types but provides no real dramatic tension.

The only conflict in the play stems from Ignacio's rediscovered love for Mercedes after she returns to Madrid. Like Pilar of *To Wake Up and Die*, Mercedes refuses to consider an adulterous relationship and leaves for South America. At this point in the play, the action departs from the novel which serves as its model. Desire to throw off the joyless war years leads to a rose colored view of reality observable in Flora's characterization and in the resolution of the sentimental conflict. Initially portrayed as an egotistical pleasure seeker, along the lines of Eva in *To Wake Up and Die*, she comes to value her husband's love; but in contrast to her predecessor, her change in character occurs with neither preparation nor explanation. Flora's case also differs in that she successfully wins back her husband's love. Here, Concha Espina resolves the love triangle: Mercedes will continue to be Ignacio's inspiration, the "divine spark" that enlightens his physical and spiritual blindness but Flora will provide the human compassion and warmth that prevents the spark from dying out. In the end, the desire to rid the play of tragic overtones prevails over Concha Espina's personal view of life.

The description of contemporary social reality is similarly devoid of conflict. The war itself is mentioned only briefly as the cause of Ignacio's blindness and a partial explanation for his broken engagement. The economic chaos characterizing postwar Spain is nowhere suggested. On the contrary, Ignacio and his family live extremely well, though journalism in Spain is not a particularly remunerative occupation even in the most favorable circumstances. In nearly every respect, *Enlightened Darkness* typifies the postwar tendency to evade the real issues, be they social or psychological. Reasonably well written, at times humorous, it is more of interest for what it omits than for what it affirms. It should be noted that during this period Concha Espina herself, like the play's protagonist, has permanently lost her eyesight. This handicap in addition to her age, seventy-one, and contemporary pressure for conformity more than suffice to explain her literary decline. Amazingly, however, artistic deterioration is not a permanent feature of her postwar literature. When many other authors would abandon their literary career, Espina somehow summons the energy and the inspiration to produce nine more volumes, among which a fair number are both interesting and artistically valuable.

III *The Lingering Effects of the War*

Concha Espina's renewed interest in the theater produces two more works, *La otra* [The other one] and *Moneda blanca* [White coin], neither of which is included in her *Complete Works*[1] and

neither is of outstanding literary value. However, both plays represent a move towards the portrayal of limited conflict. *The Other One*
constitutes her first attempt to construct a social ideal for postwar
Spain. The first two acts take place in the elegant Madrid apartment
of a young couple: Carmen, a retired actress of illegitimate birth, and
Javier, the aviator son of an aristocratic family. Unaware that the
couple is married, Javier's father Fidel still hopes that his son will
abandon Carmen and choose a wife from the upper classes. When he
learns that Carmen is in fact legally married to Javier and that she is
expecting his child, Fidel disinherits his son. In Concha Espina's
view, Fidel errs not in his aristocratic principles but in his identification of individual merit with social class. Previously, Fidel had
opposed the marriage of his daughter Fidela to Manolo, the son of a
theater manager. The reasons are the same but the justice of his
position varies greatly in the two cases. Coincidentally, Manolo's
father is Carmen's exmanager and long-time friend. Through Carmen, Manolo reestablishes his contact with Fidela and in the course
of the play the nature of their relationship is contrasted with that of
Carmen and Javier.

Manolo is motivated solely by economic interest and Fidela by an
unhealthy passion that prevails over her personal pride and her
concern for her father's values. Carmen's only desire is to prove
worthy of her husband's love and his name and to somehow effect a
reconciliation between Javier and his father. Convinced that nobility
"has always produced the best fruits," Carmen feels strongly that
privilege implies responsibilities. Fidela's willingness to marry Manolo in spite of the knowledge that his only interest is financial is, in
Carmen's view, a lamentable departure from the dignity and self-
restraint that have become intrinsic to Spanish nobility over the
course of the centuries.

For both Carmen and Javier, this tradition represents Spain's
contribution to world culture and must be upheld with an almost
religious fervor. In Javier's words, Spain is "the spiritual treasure of
the world, the human reserve of the best ideas, the apex of the most
exquisite and most generous sentiments. We should pronounce her
name on our knees."[2] Although Carmen and Fidel both equate
personal merit with noble origins, Concha Espina specifically refutes
a categorical identification of the two terms. When Javier dies in an
airplane accident, Carmen's true worth becomes apparent. Determined to reserve Javier's inheritance for their son, she requests
Fidel's permission to return to the theater in order to support herself.

In addition, she offers to share her earnings with Fidel. The contrast between Carmen's dignity and Fidela's shameful conduct is not lost on Fidel, who admits in the end that all roads can lead to God. He now accepts Carmen as the true embodiment of the values that his own daughter has rejected.

On the surface, *The Other One* represents a vindication of the novelist's contention that Spanish society has always respected individual merit more than social status. This would appear to signify a retraction of the classist rhetoric employed in the war novels and Concha Espina clearly intends to demonstrate her support for a democratization of postwar Spanish society. The shift is, however, extremely moderate. Consciously or subconsciously, she undermines her thesis by suggesting that Carmen's father was in fact of noble lineage. Although the play succeeds in demonstrating that aristocratic origin does not necessarily guarantee noble behavior, as in Fidela's case, it fails to show that individuals of common blood are capable of noble actions. The effects of the war thus continue to linger both in ideology and in rhetoric even when the intent is to move towards new social structures.

IV *Franco Spain and Catholic Rhetoric*

With respect to artistic value, *White Coin* is inferior to *The Other One* but it is the first postwar work in which political considerations *per se* recede to an almost imperceptible level. Unfortunately, in this case religious thesis replaces political partisanship and the net result is equally detrimental to literary quality. *White Coin* is essentially a dramatized *folletín* with a moral lesson. The action is unduly complicated by multiple interconnections among the characters and hints at an occult tragedy that is not revealed until the third and final act.

As Isabel—the protagonist—has always suspected, the tragedy concerns her mother's death and is related to her father's subsequent marriage to Eugenia. Although the hostility between Eugenia and Isabel's father, Leonardo, has been brewing for years, it does not cause an open rift until the moment described in the play. The unexplained breakdown of this relationship constitutes one of the major weaknesses of the play. Although Concha Espina attributes Eugenia's open animosity to her jealousy of Matilde, a former girlfriend of Leonardo's and a frequent visitor to the family home, the text indicates that this is not a new development.

Whatever the causes, Eugenia determines to reveal the long-silenced mystery in order to destroy Leonardo, Matilde, and Isabel. As it is finally revealed, the story would make excellent script for a soap opera. Incited in great part by Eugenia, Isabel's mother had an affair which Eugenia then purposely disclosed to Leonardo. Hoping that Leonardo would later marry her, Eugenia hid him in a closet with a loaded gun and arranged matters so that he would discover his wife's infidelity and shoot her in a moment of rage. Eugenia's plan succeeds in all respects except that Leonardo never legally marries her. After nineteen years of blackmail, she now feels that she has lost control and reveals all to Isabel on the eve of the girl's marriage.

In conjunction with the contrived plot, Concha Espina elaborates a moral thesis based on Isabel's evolution. Initially characterized as a somewhat frivolous, uncultured girl whom Eugenia has educated without religious or moral guidance, Isabel is strongly influenced by Matilde and her fiancé José Luis. According to the latter, it is each individual's responsibility to better his or her lot in life. In the end, Isabel adopts this principle when she decides to enter a convent so that she can repay her parents' debt to the world and to God. Although the stage directions indicate that the dramatic representation should be effected in a moderate tone, with no exaggeration, the play is essentially melodramatic, with logic being constantly sacrificed to dramatic effect. Isabel's sudden religious conversion does not follow naturally from the events unless one assumes that moral restitution is only possible within the confines of a nunnery. Despite *White Coin*'s political neutrality, the play continues to reflect a desire for conformity, in this case with the radically Catholic character of Franco Spain.

V   *The Rediscovery of Sentiment*

In 1942, Concha Espina publishes *El fraile menor* [The youngest monk], a collection of short stories written between 1920 and 1942. The return to prewar writings perhaps indicates a need to reexperience the feelings that inspired her during that period, and so resume the literary course diverted by the outbreak of hostilities. The only story actually written in 1942 does represent a departure from the immediately preceding works, echoing the tone as well as the artistic intent of her prewar stories. The change is visible as the reader progresses through the four sections of the book.

Section one, "Concerning Love," includes seven stories originally published in *The Prince of Song*, all of which reflect the author's often-stated belief that life and in particular the amorous experience generally give rise to profound disillusionment. Although the characters are frequently doomed to a life of unhappiness, their loyalty to the ideals which occasion their disillusionment and the nobility with which they endure their suffering provide a sense of peace that those responsible for their condition can never attain. In keeping with this view, Concha Espina infuses these stories with a lyrical quality transforming despair into a poignant acceptance of destiny.

The poignant element persists in the second section, "Concerning Wonder," providing emotional support for the discussion of various social realities. Never entirely absent from Concha Espina's work, social commentary and criticism are more frequent in those published after 1920. In this facet of her writing, the emphasis shifts from the exaltation of passive resignation to a sympathetic portrayal and at times active endorsement of resistance. Moderate in comparison to some of the novelist's prewar works, the stories in "Concerning Wonder" all depict individuals who merit attention because they transcend accepted standards of conduct. *"El niño en los brazos"* ["Babe in arms"] relates the story of a middle-aged widow who adopts an abandoned infant much to her neighbor's surprise. In what Espina regards as a reward for her charity, the widow subsequently receives a letter from her long-absent son who is returning from America in good health and with his hard-earned fortune. Previously unpublished, "Babe in Arms" was probably written before the Civil War but the fact that the story extols the rural lower class indicates that Concha Espina's disillusionment with this group has abated somewhat.

Also published for the first time in *The Youngest Monk, "Paloma en Nueva York"* ["Paloma in New York"] reflects the novelist's disgust at racial prejudice in the United States. The story is a sentimental and sometimes patronizing description of a young Jamaican elevator boy who befriends a three-year-old Spanish visitor to New York and bravely rescues her from a fire that breaks out in the hotel. Probably written in the early 1930's, after Espina's visit to the United States, the story's publication in 1942 indicates further concern for members of the lower classes.

The intent of the four previously unpublished war stories in "Concerning War" is more political than literary. It should be noted,

however, that the strident tone of *Red Moon* and other works of
Nationalist exaltation is less noticeable in these selections. The
characters are not symbols but individuals who experience the war in
a very personal way, each enduring the loss of something personally
valuable; a father, a walnut tree, a baby book. With the exception of
"La torre verde" ["The green tower"], the stories concern only those
who suffer the loss, not those who occasion it. The absence of the
enemy is artistically beneficial, eliminating the polarized characterization which is a frequent weakness in Concha Espina's art. Excessive
sentimentality is equally destructive to literary quality, but in the
context of Espina's previous works, it signifies a healthy regression to
a sensitivity grounded in human rather than political considerations.

The renewed concern for the victims of suffering, irrespective of
social class and (to a limited degree) of political affiliation can be seen
in "Concerning Candor," the final section of the volume. In two of the
stories previously published, the novelist demonstrates compassion
for the impoverished rural Spaniard. "Marilis," the final selection in
The Youngest Monk, and the only one actually written around the
time of publication, is the first sample of Espina's postwar writing to
have artistic effect as its principal goal. The story describes the
mysterious disappearance of a beautiful, spirited little girl who is
summering on the Spanish seashore with wealthy relatives while her
exiled parents, "absented from Spain due to sad political activities"
(*OC*, II, 813) remain in France. Marilis is abducted by a passenger on
a ship from Breton, motivated apparently by an irresistible attraction
to the child. Marilis is later recovered by the local authorities in the
first French port at which the ship stops. Miraculously, it is in this
same port that her real parents are living.

The story line is hardly noteworthy except that Concha Espina
infuses Marilis with a delightfully evanescent quality that makes the
fairy tale ending seem natural. "Marilis" contains no message, other
than a comment on the strange quirks of fate, which in itself is a
refreshing change. The fact that Concha Espina draws an engaging
portrait of the daughter of Republican exiles, with no further allusion
to political matters, indicates a renewed concern for art over and
above ideological considerations. With *The Youngest Monk*, Concha
Espina takes an important step toward resumption of her literary
course. The artistically destructive impact of the Civil War will
reappear in some of her final works but never again totally subordinate art.

VI   *Poetry in the Final Years*

Concha Espina's third and final volume of poetry appears in 1943 and is reedited in her *Complete Works* together with several poems written after that date. As previously mentioned, her value as a poet is limited and *La segunda mies* [The second crop] does not disprove this judgment. Thematically, the poems repeat concerns of *Between the Night and the Sea* with the addition of several war inspired compositions. Nature, religious devotion, and solitude provide the remaining themes. With respect to the introspective poetry, Concha Espina seems generally more at peace with herself. Although she continues to write of her sentimental tragedy, the proximity of death and liberation seems to mitigate her sense of loss. Stylistically, *The Second Crop* reflects the verbal simplicity increasingly frequent in her final works. Always reminiscent of Bécquer in certain thematic aspects, she now adopts the natural, seemingly spontaneous expression characteristic of his poetry, which reappears in her last novels.

VII   *The Transition to the Final Novels*

The promise to write a sequel to *Yesterday's Flower,* stated in the final pages of that novel, is finally fulfilled in 1944 with the publication of *Victoria en América* [Victoria in America]. The continuation of Victoria García's story confirms Espina's desire to resume her prewar course as does the fact that in this novel, the development of fictional character predominates over discussion of the war and the years immediately preceding it. Nationalist rhetoric is reduced to a relatively minor element. Similarly, the characters continue to be symbolic but retain a greater measure of individuality in comparison with their immediate predecessors. With Victoria, Concha Espina constructs a contemporary version of Spanish womanhood, adapting the qualities of many previous heroines to the historical moment. Victoria's belief that love requires a total and permanent commitment between two individuals leads her to reject the sexual freedom and romantic inconstancy that she observes in the United States. As Miguelina Velez's secretary, she accompanies her on a lecture tour through North and South America that retraces Concha Espina's itineraries of 1928 and 1935. Victoria's visits to New York, Middlebury, and other unnamed localities of the United States enable the novelist to contrast the moral character of her protagonist with that of the local women. With a natural elegance that spurns makeup, the latest fashion, and all but the simplest adornment, Victoria's unorthodox beauty attracts the attention of all.

Identically dressed, intellectually superficial, culturally deficient, and indiscriminate with their sexual favors, Victoria's female admirers in New York are only slightly less insufferable than Glen Parks, Lorenzo Alcaín's first wife who reappears in *Victoria in America*. Victoria's defense of absolute love and of profound commitment, be it political, moral or spiritual, is lost on these women whose only interest is the pursuit of immediate gratification. Victoria's superiority is demonstrated by the intense but pure devotion that she inspires in her male acquaintances. No fewer than thirteen men fall in love with her in the course of the novel, including two Middlebury professors who only vaguely perceive her true value but realize that it is vastly superior to that of the women in the United States.

The one-dimensional characterization of North American women and the contrived disposition of the action to confirm Victoria's preeminence in all aspects of her personality are glaring defects in the novel. Nevertheless, if the reader disregards this obvious stacking of the deck and focuses solely on Victoria's personality, she comes across as a spirited, appealing human being. Espina's discussion of Victoria does not coincide entirely with what Victoria reveals herself to be. Victoria's version proves considerably more interesting as well as convincing, in terms of human psychology, than does the novelist's. By her actions, Victoria discloses the emotional immaturity of adolescence. Forced by her abnormal childhood and early adolescence to assume a self-sufficiency that does not reflect true maturity, Victoria prematurely identifies the fulfillment of her personal destiny with marriage to Lorenzo Alcaín. Her Romantic view of the world leads her to see the twice-repeated convergence of their paths as proof of predestined union.

With characteristic impetuosity, Victoria leaves for America not really clear about the purpose of her journey but anxious to prove herself worthy of Lorenzo's love. Gradually, the realization that she has no definite goals and the growing self-doubts with respect to the desirability of a marriage to Lorenzo transform her into a moody, and at times petulant, individual. Her actions belie descriptions of a saintly, exceedingly self-restrained young girl. Spontaneous and anxious to possess the happiness that she believes rightfully hers, Victoria resents Lorenzo's altruistic subordination of their personal interests to the Nationalist cause. She never fully resigns herself to his decision to remain in Spain although rationally, she comprehends the merit of his position. Her discontent is intensified by a growing recognition that her vitality conflicts with the qualities that Lorenzo admires in a woman. Victoria intuitively senses his love for Engracia and although she admires her aunt greatly, rebels against the possibility that her own life might follow a course similar to her aunt's.

It is hard to imagine that Victoria could ever reconcile herself to Engracia's belief that life is suffering and that the proper attitude is one of serene, passive resignation. The difference between the two women is much more than difference in age. Temperamentally, Victoria is an adventurous, spirited, rebellious individual. Her refusal to accept the Quintaval name and accompanying financial security, her aggressive defense of her ideals, the episode in which she slaps Glen Parks in the face, and her general spontaneity all indicate a character less suited to marriage with Lorenzo than with Emilio Santillán, the impetuous, at times arrogant, but basically admirable ship's officer whom Victoria meets on her trip across the Atlantic. Subconsciously aware that Emilio has gradually displaced Lorenzo in her affections, Victoria continues to honor her initial commitment, reluctant to admit that she is capable of any romantic inconstancy. Miguelina's preference for Lorenzo contributes also. Ultimately, Lorenzo's death during the Civil War frees Victoria from what would probably have been an unsuitable marriage.

Emilio's character, like Victoria's, demonstrates a convincing combination of contradictory qualities. He has a youthful faith in his ability to create his own happiness which attracts Victoria when she contrasts it to Lorenzo's identification of life and suffering. Emilio's confidence is vindicated, as with Miguelina's blessings, he marries Victoria and all indications point to a happy life together. The uncharacteristically happy ending is in keeping with the nature of the central characters. Unlike most of Concha Espina's male figures, Emilio is clearly delineated and shown to be ideally suited to Victoria.

Unfortunately, the attempt to make Victoria and Emilio symbols of national character weakens their otherwise excellent characterization. The same holds true for the minor figures, who range from unacceptable stereotypes to potentially interesting characters that remain insufficiently developed. More important for what they reveal about Victoria than as representatives of human personality, they lack the human dimension that makes secondary characters valuable in any work of art. In spite of their incompleteness, they reflect a renewed interest by the novelist in the diversity of human types and the conflicts that this diversity engenders. César Bustamente, Agustín Linares, Gomes García, and Jaroslav Rezek all indicate a degree of psychological insight not apparent in the preceding works and more fully exploited in those that follow.

Ideologically, *Victoria in America* reiterates attitudes or beliefs already expressed in other works. The exaltation of Hispanic values, the negative view of the United States, the conviction that Spain has a crucial role to play in the cultural and moral evolution of Latin America, all appear early in her writing and are restated here in conjunction with Falangist ideology. Like the presentation of character, the enunciation of ideological premises is not always consistent with the novelistic action. Victoria's insistence that love for the Spanish woman represents a total and irrevocable commitment to a single individual is not borne out by her behavior.

Similarly, the attempt to categorize individuals according to national origin or political affiliation fails in the cases of César Bustamente and Agustín Linares. César is a young man who was blinded by his friend Agustín in a hunting accident. Anxious to somehow compensate for his error, Agustín had offered to serve as César's companion on a trip to America; but after a short period, Agustín finds himself increasingly resentful. Agustín, ambitious and self-centered, fears that his absence from Spain will permanently damage his career. For his part, César plays on Agustín's sense of guilt to ensure his constant companionship. Blindness has intensified his tendency for self-pity and envy, creating constant conflict between the two men. During one altercation aboard the ship, Agustín explodes in anger and purposely pushes César into the ocean. The incident occurs at night and no one is informed that César has disappeared until it is too late to attempt a rescue.

Both men represent the destructive egotism generally associated with Spain's cultural and political antagonists. The inconsistency could be interpreted as an indication of Espina's growing independence from partisan art if she did not go to such extreme lengths to rationalize César's insufferable self-indulgence and his murder at Agustín's hand. As the creator of realistic psychological types, Concha Espina has succeeded in throwing off the one-dimensional perspective imposed by the war but she is still unable to accept the ideological implications of her approach. Consequently, she attempts to reconcile evidence with a preconceived set of principles that do not apply to the case in question.

Stylistically, *Victoria in America* reflects the transitional ideological character of the novel. The conventional rhetoric of the preceding works alternates with a natural expression that compares favorably with the best of Concha Espina's prose. She excels in the recreation of small talk which appears to convey nothing but, in fact, reveals a great deal about the conversant parties. Generally she tends to eliminate this aspect of human speech in favor of a more intense dialogue. In *Victoria in America,* Concha Espina combines the two forms of discourse and as a result, the dialogue simulates genuine human communication to a degree not often found in her novels. Despite its obvious defects, *Victoria in America* represents an important moment in Concha Espina's career. At seventy-five, after a long lapse in artistic achievement, she reveals an unexpected resurgence of creative energy that will attain full force in her next novel.

CHAPTER 9

The Final Novels

I A New Approach to Fiction in the Final Years

CONCHA Espina's third to last novel represents a departure from her previous work in a number of ways. Whereas she has formerly limited her representation of the male-female relationship to the discovery of love or the attempt to reconstruct a meaningful life following sentimental disillusionment, *El más fuerte* [The strongest one] concentrates on the pressures and psychological realities that accompany the gradual dissolution of the amorous bond. With the exception of isolated short stories, *The Strongest One* is the first of Concha Espina's publications in which a male character is the protagonist. Both of these innovations persist in her last two novels, as does the analysis of the individual in relationship with the various components of the family unit.

The novel tells the story of Adrián Montaves and the people who influence and are influenced by him. All are portrayed simultaneously as unique individuals and as members of their social group.[1] The collective character of the novel predominates in the first part where Concha Espina slowly introduces Adrián's family and friends, his wife Magdalena, their three children, Adrián's brother and sister, the children's friends, Magdalena's mother, and Adrián's law partner. The initial description of the novelistic cast simulates the superficial impression of an external observer who may perceive some hint of conflict but generally fails to penetrate the family structure.

Married for eighteen years, Adrián and Magdalena are to all appearances a happy couple who have been blessed with economic prosperity and three healthy, beautiful children. Although Magdalena is the illegitimate daughter of a poor seamstress, she has assimilated the manners and refinement of her husband's socially superior family, largely through the guidance of Paula Montaves,

Adrián's deceased mother. It was doña Paula who originally brought Magdalena into the family home as a young dressmaker and it was she who insisted that Adrián marry the girl when she learned that Magdalena was carrying Adrián's child. Deeply in love, Adrián willingly complied and for the next eighteen years no sign of serious marital conflict emerged. Two years after the "premature" birth of Asunción, Magdalena gives birth to twins, Rosario and Pablo. At the time of her death, doña Paula has every reason to believe that her intervention has assured the happiness of her youngest son and the social as well as moral reeducation of her daughter-in-law. However, as Adrián comes to admit, his relationship with Magdalena has never faced the test of adversity and only in various trials does the true character of both Adrián and Magdalena fully come to light.

Always somewhat insecure of her position within the Montaves family and consequently overly sensitive to any suggestion of personal shortcomings, Magdalena jealously defends her authority as wife and mother. At the same time, she is unwilling to accept blame for any failure occuring within her sphere of responsibility. With three children at various stages of adolescence, the problems confronting Magdalena become increasingly complex and like many parents, she and Adrián are not always able to meet the challenge. The sudden and at times violent emancipation of the Montaves children inevitably strains the family bonds; but whereas Adrián ultimately rises to the occasion, Magdalena neither comprehends nor acknowledges the true significance of her children's behavior.

The first indication of family conflict is revealed in the opening pages of the novel although the full impact of the incident does not become apparent until much later. In a rare manifestation of marital dissension, Adrián and Magdalena find themselves radically opposed concerning their daughter Asunción's first romantic relationship. Invariably anxious to ensure her children's love for her, Magdalena defends Asunción's flirtation with Manolo Cedrún in spite of Adrián's reminder that Manolo is engaged to marry the daughter of family friends. Although Asunción appears to resign herself to her father's opposition, her behavior continues to mystify the family and only reverts to normalcy when she becomes engaged to Gonzalo Artola, Adrián's young law partner. While Asunción appears to be moving towards a healthy adjustment to her circumstances, the normally vivacious Rosario assumes a moody, dispirited manner that perplexes and worries Adrián. Although Magdalena correctly theorizes that Rosario is in love with Gonzalo, Adrián becomes too involved with his other children to pursue the matter. His son Pablo has been associating with Martín Valero, a Communist of questionable character and Adrián fears that the influence is not healthy. In fact, Martín is encouraging Pablo to abandon his studies in a military academy and compromise his young girl friend so that the families will be forced to permit their marriage.

Throughout the various major and minor crises, Magdalena supports her children's whims and rejects Adrián's attempts to guide them toward more mature behavior. When Asunción disappears with the now married Manolo Cedrún during the party celebrating her own engagement to Gonzalo, Magdalena's first reaction is to blame Adrián for originally opposing his daughter's marriage to Manolo. Similarly, when Pablo insists on abandoning the military career that he and his mother originally chose in spite of Adrián's opposition, Magdalena sides with her son. She refuses to accept Adrián's view that Pablo should not be permitted to capriciously drop his career. Overcome by the emotional turmoil that accompanies adolescence, Pablo commits suicide, leaving his father with grave doubts as to the wisdom of his position and his mother convinced that Adrián has once more been the cause of her children's misfortune.

Throughout the novel, the narration of the various family crises is presented from Adrián's perspective. Consequently, Magdalena's character is not fully revealed until the later parts of *The Strongest One*. At this point, Adrián's love no longer impedes an objective appraisal and Magdalena's actions have provided an adequate basis for the reader's evaluation. As a result, the story produces a sense of discovery rarely present in Concha Espina's works which contributes greatly to the novel's interest. Although indications of Magdalena's less than admirable character are introduced in the early chapters through statements of Eduardo, Adrián's brother, Espina wisely refrains from corroborating this negative evaluation. As a priest, Eduardo judges individuals with a severity that overlooks the multiple shadings of human relationships. Consequently, his vision is not necessarily accurate. His appraisal of Magdalena serves as one of many clues in the total reconstruction of her personality, a labor that requires the active participation of the reader throughout the novel.

Adrián's psychological identity is revealed in a similar fashion. Characterized by his mother as "the strongest one," his life history has convinced family and friends that he is, in fact, exceptionally self-assured and resolute in his decisions. Magdalena herself alludes sarcastically to his inflexibility when she remarks that he always speaks as one who gives orders. Adrián's strength, however, is a myth, as he discovers to his own amazement. It is only in the course of the novel that he acquires a real direction in life, which in his case, necessitates the gradual loss of his affection for Magdalena.

With his wife's happiness and that of their children at stake, Adrián is torn between his own sense of moral rectitude and Magdalena's defense of questionable behavior. He gradually discovers that his love for Magdalena is based on half truths that he has cultivated in order to preserve the illusion of happiness. In the end, Adrián is forced to admit that his attempts to salvage past happiness have prevented him from attending to his professional and paternal responsibilities. Ultimately, Adrián's strength lies in his ability to accept failure whereas Magdalena clings to a hope that the past can be relived; Asunción's honor will somehow be reinstated and Adrián's alienation is not to be a permanent state.

Adrián now turns his attention to the present and to the reconstruction of a future based on the irrevocable events which have transpired. His effort to restore Rosario's vitality on the heels of the family tragedies marks the first step towards his own rehabilitation. Already showing signs of recovery, Rosario's zest for life is fully revived with the unexpected return of Gonzalo Artolo, last seen on the fateful night when Asunción disappeared with Manolo. Gonzalo's timely return and his sudden confession of love for Rosario stretch the limits of credibility, but in all other respects the description of their romance is delightfully executed. In contrast to many of Concha Espina's female characters, Rosario's love is not dehumanized with excessive references to the Romantic ideal. Like Victoria of the preceding novel, she retains an almost childish spontaneity that does not exclude a sentimental maturity. Impetuous, refreshingly nonconformist in some of her attitudes, she is at the same time exceptionally perceptive in her appraisal of human relationships and psychologically well adjusted. Rosario's exuberance and Gonzalo's more subdued but genuine happiness confirm Adrián's conviction that all happiness is not illusory and that the experiences of the past must not be allowed to hinder the elaboration of new forms of existence. With a sense of purpose that is at long last an integral part of his character, Adrián informs Magdalena that he no longer loves her and departs for America where Asunción—now abandoned and pregnant—awaits him.

Unlike many of Concha Espina's novels, there is no moral in *The Strongest One*. With the exception of the one-dimensional charac-

terization of Martín Valero, she concentrates fully on the peculiarities
of the human psyche and the many variables that determine human
relationships. She is closer to Galdós in this novel than in any of her
works, both in the emphasis on the social group and the absence of a
fixed vision with respect to the materials presented. It is the reader,
not the author, who ultimately judges the characters. To this end,
Concha Espina relies heavily on dialogue, description of conduct,
and interior monologue, all employed with an appearance of spontaneity not always present in her writing. Stylistically, the novel
exhibits a continued interest in clarity as opposed to verbal enrich-
ment of the language. The expression simulates that of colloquial
discourse with its emphasis on immediate comprehension over
rhetorical excellence. *The Strongest One* is notable for the elimina-
tion of the hyperbole that all too frequently mars her work. Seventy-
eight years old and totally blind, Espina produces a novel that rivals
the best of her writing in its expression and disposition of the action,
and surpasses all but one or two in the analysis of human psychology.

II   *Regionalism and a Fresh Look at the Problem of Rape*

Concha Espina's second to last novel is dedicated to the land and
sea of her native Santander. Appropriately entitled *Un valle en el mar*
[A valley in the sea], it aspires to capture the human and physical
peculiarities of the region. In this and other respects, the novel
continues the Regionalist literature of Pereda, named in the book as
one of the foremost chroniclers of the area. The similarity with Pereda
goes beyond the description of local custom, geographical setting,
and native types. For both authors, Cantabria exemplifies a social
ideal and its people embody the values that they personally endorse.[2]
Although regionalism and traditionalism are two distinct phenomena, their boundaries are not always discernible either in Pereda
or in Concha Espina.

Like Pereda's *Sotileza, A Valley in the Sea* upholds the class
divisions of Cantabrian society as natural and immutable. Notwithstanding Espina's insistence on the democratic character of the
community and the illustrious ancestry of the local people, the
characters themselves actively perpetuate a rigidly stratified society.
Conflict arises only when the prevailing structure is threatened and
resolves itself when equilibrium is restored. The novel's protagonist
also reflects Pereda's influence: Salvadora, like Sotileza, is a rare
combination of spontaneity and reserve, peasant simplicity and more

cultured refinement. In both cases, complex psychology is insinuated but not fully illuminated, leaving the reader with a sense of the enigmatic, impenetrable quality of human personality.

While ideological bias affects both *Sotileza* and *A Valley in the Sea*, Espina's novel is considerably less overt in this aspect. Whereas the central issue in the nineteenth century work is the reestablishment of social equilibrium, in Salvadora's story the main focus falls on the issue of rape and its consequences in a rural, socially stratified community. Abandoned as an infant, Salvadora is subsequently adopted by Pedro and Eduvigis Granda. The Grandas have always wanted a daughter but have given up all hope after the birth of their seventh son. From the beginning, Eduvigis dreams that some day Salvadora will marry one of the Granda boys and so become a true member of the family.

Outwardly acquiescent, Salvadora's true feelings with respect to her future remain an enigma for fellow townspeople and reader alike. Conversing with the Mother Superior of the school where she was educated, she bitterly remarks that Pedro Granda has never been a father to her, suggesting that she harbors some hopes of a more illustrious ancestry which would entitle her to a husband of higher rank. Nevertheless, when she reaches marriageable age, her only resistance appears in her adamant refusal to consider Antonio, the oldest Granda son. Instead, she chooses Ricardo, the second in the line of potential husbands. According to local gossip, Salvadora is not in love with her fiancé and chooses him only to gain time, knowing that his chronic liver ailment will run its course before their marriage can be celebrated.

In the opening pages of the novel, Ricardo succumbs to his illness and Salvadora is left to choose once more among the remaining Granda sons. Her enigmatic character and the unique circumstances of her life intrigue all those acquainted with her story, including Julio Rosales—the town mayor—and his houseguest, Fermín Abascal. A noted psychiatrist, Abascal initially finds the case interesting from a professional standpoint but in the ensuing days, his interest becomes increasingly personal. Strangely mesmerized by the girl appropriately nicknamed "Siren," Abascal abruptly declares his love to the astonished Salvadora and subsequently rapes her while escorting her home from the Rosales' manor.

Initially, Espina's analysis of Abascal's character reveals a high degree of psychological insight. Outwardly dispassionate, as conditioned by his scientific background, he has long sublimated deep-seated impulses that are abruptly triggered by the change in physical and emotional environment. Shocked to discover a previously unsuspected facet of his personality and mortified to confess his social and moral transgression, Abascal makes no mention of the incident until subsequent events force him to seek Julio Rosales' advice.

Salvadora's reaction to the rape is similarly effective. Temporarily stupefied by the sheer brutality of the act, she gradually comes to the full realization of her situation. Her first impulse to escape through suicide is followed by an overwhelming desire to continue the life she has only briefly experienced. Finally, she comes to a rebellious insistence on her own innocence and a deep hatred for Abascal. For the present, she too decides to keep the incident a secret. On Salvadora's return to the Granda home, she is met by Basilio, the fifth of Eduvigis' sons and Salvadora's childhood favorite. Basilio's warm welcome and concern for her poorly disguised anguish now signify the possibility of a safe refuge to the distraught girl. Her monosyllabic acceptance of Basilio's sudden marriage proposal provides no clue as to her real feelings. Although she later speaks of a long-standing preference for Basilio and a hope that he would return from military service in time to prevent her marriage to Ricardo, it is not clear whether her love for him is a spontaneous emotion or an outgrowth of her need for a safe harbor.

Always mindful of the possible consequences of her rape, Salvadora tacitly encourages Basilio's impatience to set a wedding date. Although she welcomes their marriage as a solution to her increasingly evident pregnancy, she also finds herself more and more reluctant to deceive him. The few individuals who are party to her secret propose that she conform to the conventional standards for such cases and marry Abascal. The Mother Superior to whom Salvadora turns for advice, Leonor Rosales, and Abascal himself all believe that Abascal is morally bound to rectify his malefaction and that Salvadora is equally bound to accept his restitution. When Salvadora rebels against the unjust disenfranchisement of her already violated rights to personal happiness, Mother Socorro secretly comments that "this child doesn't reason as God wills, she isn't in her right mind" (*OC*, II, 159). For his part, Abascal arrogantly declares that by virtue of his forced physical possession, Salvadora belongs to him and to him alone.

In the light of traditional attitudes towards the rape victim, Salvadora's refusal to marry Abascal and her insistence on her right to pursue a course more favorable to her personal happiness represent a declaration of emancipation that is doomed to failure. Although her marriage to Basilio enables her to forestall the inevitable, the birth of a healthy, fullterm son after seven months of marriage leaves little hope for continued happiness. Up to this point in the novel, the presentation of the characters' conflicts and motives is without fault. The choice of rape as a central issue is in itself noteworthy in contemporary Spanish literature and Concha Espina's analysis of its implications is extremely well thought out. Unfortunately, the second half of the novel does not sustain the same level of artistic quality.

While the characterization of Antonio, the rejected oldest Granda son, and Salvadora continues without significant modification, for the majority of the characters, psychological complexity gives way to a one-dimensional rigidity severely undermining the novel's credibility. Basilio's naive belief that the newborn child is his own and Julio Rosales' dramatic discovery that his concern for Salvadora's situation is in fact, a manifestation of romantic passion are absurdly unrealistic. The same is true of Leonor Rosales' bizarre passion for Abascal which leads the morally impeccable woman to forgive his crime at the same time that she makes light of Salvadora's undeniable anguish. All these incidents signal an unexpected deterioration in the novel that reaches bottom with a revised portrait of Fermín Abascal in the latter half of the story.

Initially described as an example of the tenuous balance between instinct and intellect, Abascal's motives and conduct are complex but comprehensible. Following Salvadora's marriage to Basilio, Abascal's character undergoes a radical and unexplained transformation. As his psychological complexity decreases, his motivation becomes increasingly obscure. Basilio's discovery of his deception could plausibly come from a number of sources; but inexplicably it is Abascal who reveals the truth in a letter that does not seem to have any real purpose. Again, when Basilio is killed in an airplane accident after fleeing from home, Abascal's visit to the Granda house and his cruel revelation of the truth to Eduvigis have no apparent explanation. The shock kills Eduvigis and arbitrarily complicates the novelistic action. Since there is no discussion of Abascal's mental state during this period, it is impossible to know if he is totally deranged, sadistically intent on destroying Salvadora, or somehow convinced that his actions will in the end ensure his marriage to Salvadora. The motives of Salvadora's real father, who allies himself with Abascal and conspires with him to abduct Salvadora's son, are similarly obscure.

These gaps and inconsistencies as well as the lengthy, uninteresting descriptions of local history constitute major weaknesses that are only partially compensated by the successful execution of other facets in the novel. Gerardo Diego's view that *A Valley in the Sea* represents one of Concha Espina's very best novels[3] can be accepted only if applied selectively to limited portions of the book. The descriptions of the Cantabrian countryside are at times extremely effective. However, Espina frequently departs from the central action to dwell excessively on the historical and cultural significance of the region. In my judgment, the outstanding merit of the novel lies in the portrait of Antonio and to a lesser extent, in that of Salvadora.

Torn between his love for Salvadora, his jealousy, pity, and love for Basilio, and his concern for the family honor, Antonio's initial intervention is necessarily limited. He can only observe from a distance as the events gradually unfold and enable him to intervene in a more active manner. Although he believes that Salvadora in no way provoked her own rape, traditional attitudes towards the dishonored woman prevent him from revealing this opinion to her. Salvadora looks on him with fear as the severe guardian of the Granda name but Concha Espina corrects this vision with a number of details that reveal a deep tenderness. Salvadora herself gradually comes to recognize Antonio's true character. Basilio's death represents the final link in the chain of events that begins with her rape. At first, Salvadora sees only the repetition of the tragic pattern that has governed her life but after a long period of depression, she realizes that the tragedy has played itself out. She now turns to Antonio as the only individual capable of accepting her as she is and constructing a new life of happiness with her.

Antonio's unquestioning acceptance of Salvadora's abrupt marriage proposal is characteristic of his personality. Outwardly inexpressive, he is essentially a warm, generous individual. His characterization hinges on a number of conflicting impulses and external pressures, all of which Concha Espina delineates clearly and convincingly. Like Adrián or Magdalena of *The Strongest One*, Antonio is revealed through his conduct, speech, or gesture with no authorial judgment. In the end it is the reader who reconstructs the completed portrait and discovers one of Concha Espina's most human characters.

Salvadora's characterization is also of superior quality although the nature of her relationship with Antonio is not adequately explored. Given her initial rejection of Antonio, her discovery of growing love for him in the final paragraphs of the novel is not acceptable without some clarification of the change in attitude. Salvadora's emotional indifference after Basilio's death and her attempts to erase the memory of her tragedy with physical labor are consistent with her own character and the general pattern of human behavior, but her sudden realization that Antonio represents the key to future happiness requires more explanation if it is not to be interpreted as an arbitrary resolution of the action. A number of hypotheses suggest themselves—any of which would render Salvadora's final actions intelligible—but they cannot be applied without some supporting evidence. All too often in Espina's writing, potentially intriguing character is lost to vague allusion and sudden, unexplained deviations in behavior.

III *Concha Espina as Literary Critic*

Concha Espina's only publication approaching literary criticism appears in 1951. *De Antonio Machado a su grande y secreto amor* [From Antonio Machado to his great and secret love] reveals for the first time Antonio Machado's love affair with the still unidentified Guiomar. After Guiomar's death, a mutual friend temporarily loaned Concha Espina her letters from Machado and urged her to incorporate them in a book about the poet. The love affair is only one aspect covered in Concha Espina's study, for as she herself states, her aim is to refute the view that Machado was an atheist and a Communist. Although Concha Espina never reveals the identity of her source and he in turn refuses to identify Guiomar, there is no reason to doubt the authenticity of the letters. Unfortunately, Espina does not reproduce them in their entirety and consequently, the value of the find is less than it might be. She admits to purging the poet's adverse comments on contemporary writers and possibly also omitted or deleted other segments.

For the critic, the publication of Machado's comments on his own work and his literary aspirations are probably the most valuable contribution of Concha Espina's volume. Her analysis of the content of the letters is of limited interest except as a reflection of her own attitudes during this period. The desire to vindicate the poet's religious faith leads her to read meaning into passages that are either ambivalent or simply conventional phrases. The discussion of Machado's work without any consideration for chronology further weakens her thesis. Machado's views clearly change in the course of his life and to cite poems written in 1912 as proof of attitudes held in the 1930's is a questionable procedure. Whether Machado was in fact an atheist or a Communist is of no concern in a study of Concha Espina's writings; however, her desire to reinstate the poet to the good graces of Nationalist Spain and her comments on the Civil War warrant further attention. As stated earlier, Espina never fully liberates herself from the rhetoric of Franco Spain although time serves to moderate her initial intransigence. With respect to religious matters, the attitude revealed in her study of Machado is identical to that of her early works. Profoundly Catholic at all times, she evolves only in that the criticism of certain individuals associated with the Church disappears in her postwar writing.

Politically, the shift is more noticeable. Although Concha Espina decries Machado's treatment by the Republicans, she limits her references to the prewar and wartime political situation to a minimum. She ironically alludes to the more intransigent comments of her informant, which she prefers not to incorporate in her volume. Eleven years have now passed since the war's end and Espina's interests are clearly in other areas. In this respect, her comments on Machado's apoliticism are revealing: "NeoRomantic, in our view, and Classic in the infallible heritage of the Spanish mystics, this literary genius remains remote from the vulgar and malicious affairs of politics" (OC, II, 933). Also interesting in terms of Concha Espina's personal outlook in her final years is the emphasis on life as a positive, pleasurable experience. Her desire to counteract the popular view of a prematurely aged Machado, lost in the memories of his past with little concern for the enjoyment of the present, reflects her own shift towards a more balanced, almost optimistic view of life. In contrast to her early works, suffering is now portrayed as a constituent element in the human experience rather than as its single most important aspect. Similarly, love, even when it fails to sustain the vigor of its early stages, is seen as a positive experience that can be remembered with joy. The absolutism characterizing much of Espina's works has gradually given way to a more relativistic vision of life. The widening of horizons, dramatically halted by the Civil War, reappears in Concha Espina's final years.

IV *Love in the Final Novel*

It seems inevitable that Concha Espina's final novel be a love story. Throughout her career, she has remained faithful to the view that the novel is essentially a narrative of the amorous experience. Although in her personal life it would seem that maternal affection and professional commitment are considerably more significant than the male-female relationship, in her writing she focuses almost exclusively on the various stages of romantic love. Initially, this emphasis can be traced to her dependency on the *folletín* as well as to the somewhat circumscribed range of themes considered appropriate for a woman writer. Perhaps with more encouragement from contemporary critics and with a more assertive personality, she might have broken the repetitious thematic pattern. Despite her adherence to a single theme, there are marked changes in her treatment of the love relationship over the course of her career.

In the prologue to *Una novel de amor* [A novel of love], Concha Espina remarks that she has inopportunely written a work devoid of sin, sensual excesses, and the extravagances characteristic of the contemporary novel. The same applies partially to her early works but her accurate description of *A Novel of Love* as "a soothing book, with no clamorous virtues and with a surplus of doubt, because of the many unanswered questions it raises" (*OC*, II, 282-283) reflects a change in vision that has gradually asserted itself in her writing.

Based on Marcelino Menéndez y Pelayo's youthful romance with Conchita Pintado, the novel is a simple story of a relationship that fails to sustain itself. It does not pretend to comment on some general truth about life nor does it offer any judgment of the events it narrates; what transpires is the personal drama of individuals which can be partially reconstructed but never fully known. Both in its emphasis on the interaction between several individuals and the incorporation of the reader as final judge of the action, *A Novel of Love* represents a technical continuation of *The Strongest One*. While of lesser artistic quality on the whole than the earlier novel, parts of it equal Concha Espina's best.

The early chapters of *A Novel of Love* take place in the 1860's and describe the courtship and marriage of Conchita's parents. Agustín Pintado, a ship captain forced to seek port in the Mediterranean town of Benidorm, briefly meets there the young widow, María Llorca Pérez de Guzmán, and falls passionately in love with her. Within twenty-four hours he has introduced himself and extracted her promise to marry him on his return from the Philippines. Although the whirlwind courtship seems unrealistic, Concha Espina successfully dissipates the reader's incredulity by reminders that the episode is historically based and by frequent allusions to the seemingly implausible character of the narrative. Written in a serene, lyric language that effectively captures the idyllic quality of the relationship, the opening chapters leave the impression of a sublime but also human drama. For the first time in Concha Espina's writing, the sense of impending destiny works toward the personal happiness of the characters. As in "Boats in the Sea" or *The Rose of the Winds*, the atmosphere reflects or portends the determination of the individuals' fate; but here all aspects join to emphasize the miraculous confluence of two destinies.

Although the depiction of Agustín and María Llorca's relationship successfully captures the ecstasy of love in the moment of discovery, Concha Espina is unable to sustain the same level of artistic quality in the succeeding pages. Her attempts to recreate life on the seas in the late nineteenth century lead her to subordinate the central characters to extended and frequently uninteresting descriptions of ocean voyages or nautical customs. Dialogue virtually disappears from large segments of the novel, displaced by irrelevant comments on the cultural excellence of the period. Almost lost in the descriptive passages, the Pintado family reappears briefly when the novelist summarily refers to the births of the three Pintado children and the ongoing passion of their parents. It is only with the death of María Llorca's daughter by her first marriage that the interest level begins to rise again. Whereas the initial portrayal of Agustín and María Llorca concentrates on the extraordinary circumstances of their meeting, with little attention to their psychological makeup, Covncha Espina now subtly introduces the reader to the inner world of her characters. María Llorca's reaction to the death of her daughter reveals an emotional immaturity that has continued unchecked precisely because Agustín's love has served as a buffer against all hardship.

With the exception of her brief period as a widow, María Llorca has enjoyed a financial and emotional security that leaves her unable to cope with any sign of adversity. Forced by her daughter's death to admit the fragile basis of her own happiness, she lacks the inner resources to withstand this assault on her crisis free existence. Only through Agustín's persistent invocation of their enviable good fortune is she able to shake off her self-pitying despondency. Always treated with an unqualified deference that she comes to expect, she gradually assumes a childish egocentrism that blinds her to the suffering of others.

Agustín never wavers in his absolute devotion to his wife, yet it is clear to the reader that his desire to ensure María Llorca's happiness necessitates silencing expression of his own suffering. He suppresses his own fear of death and his conviction that he does not have long to live. His only concern is to somehow continue the protective mantle of his love even after he has died. To this end he composes a moving testimony of their life of happiness which he hides where María Llorca will find it after his death. Characteristically, his final words are a declaration of love and his final will, as expressed in the letter, is that María Llorca and their daughter Conchita continue to enjoy the happiness he has constructed for them.

It is this expression of Agustín's will, in combination with María Llorca's immature perception of life, that determines the outcome of the novel. With the third part of *A Novel of Love*, Concha Espina introduces Marcelino Menéndez y Pelayo, here portrayed as a young man on the verge of national fame. He arrives at the Pintado home in Sevilla during a professional trip to the town. Parallelling Agustín's arrival in Benidorm, Marcelino falls instantly in love with Conchita and immediately proposes marriage. For María Llorca, however, the circumstances are not the same; Marcelino's youth, his financial situation, and his idiosyncratic behavior are variants that give rise to her initial opposition. Although she apears to undergo a change of attitude, her relationship with Marcelino lacks the warmth that would substantiate her verbal approval.

With an absence of authorial judgment that is characteristic of the novel, Concha Espina barely hints at her character's true feelings until María Llorca herself openly declares her hostility. Typically, her first concern is egocentric; with childish inability to discriminate between true affection and the gratification of her desire, she explodes in anger when Marcelino naively reveals that he did not intervene in a case concerning the Pintado family. As Conchita's fiancé he felt morally obliged to abstain from voting when her brother Ignacio's application for a government position came under his jurisdiction. Although Ignacio obtains the job with no difficulty, María Llorca interprets Marcelino's conduct as a sign of less than total commitment to the family interests.

Hoping that Conchita will eventually forget Marcelino, María Llorca leads her daughter on a series of trips. From childhood, Conchita has viewed her mother with an awe that has its origins in Agustín's deferential treatment of his wife. During the present conflict, Conchita's only response is a characteristic "Yes, mamá." Time gradually does erode Conchita's passion and within two years, she marries a young lawyer-composer from Valencia. Marcelino withdraws to his research, true to his promise that if he cannot marry Conchita, he will remain a bachelor. Some twenty years later, he is surprised in his quarters in The Royal Academy of History by a visit from Conchita. Ironically, she has come to request his help in arranging a transfer for her sick husband. On this occasion, Marcelino promises to use his influence.

The description of Marcelino and Conchita's conversation after a separation of twenty years should be included among Concha Espina's best pages. The initial discomfort of both parties, the small talk punctuated by nostalgic silences, the sense of underlying warmth that continues in their relationship, and the simple but poignant farewell that marks the end to their story combine to create a moving, authentic picture of human interaction.

There is no real tragedy in *A Novel of Love*. Conchita's marriage has to all appearances been happy and Marcelino's life has been rewarding and productive. If his personal enjoyment of life could have been greater, the fault lies neither with an adverse fate nor with morally abject antagonists—as in Concha Espina's early works—but with a variety of human weaknesses that alter his course. María Llorca's well-intentioned but self-indulgent behavior, Conchita's unquestioning compliance with her mother's interpretation of life, and Marcelino's own failure to agressively seek a reconciliation must all bear the responsibility for the disunion of two individuals whose experience of life might have been richer if they had not allowed their paths to diverge.

Like the narrative of Agustín and María Llorca's relationship, that of Marcelino and Conchita is frequently interrupted by passages only loosely pertinent to the central action. At times the novel seems to be only a pretext to glorify Menéndez y Pelayo's undeniable stature as poet, historian, and critic. Whereas Concha Espina maintains a low profile in the fictionalized version of the love stories, her presence is everywhere evident in the discussion of historical or literary background. The novel's weakness is precisely this failure to maintain the boundaries between historical novel and subjective documentary. When Espina concentrates on the creation of character and plot, *A Novel of Love* reaches a level of artistic achievement seldom matched in her work; but when she lapses into interpretive analysis, her final novel betrays the hyperbolic distortion of reality that all too often impoverishes her art.

CHAPTER 10

Concha Espina:The Woman and the Novelist

O NE measure of a great artist is his or her ability to transcend the limitations imposed by personal, social, or historical circumstances. The study of Concha Espina's works demonstrates that she frequently fails in this respect. With the exception of *Mariflor, The Foundling,* major portions of *The Metal of the Dead,* a selection of short stories and sections of her remaining novels, she is not able to overcome the obstacles besetting a woman writer in the Spain of her time. It is impossible to disregard Espina's sex in a consideration of her work. Concha Espina the woman explains to a large degree Concha Espina the novelist.

The deficient education provided to the women of her period explains her dependence on art forms that have already run their course and her defective knowledge of the major intellectual movements of the time. Furthermore, Concha Espina was raised in a society that discouraged independence in women. Her initial exaltation of feminine submissiveness clearly reflects values inculcated in her from an early age. Both as a writer and as a woman, she shows a strong distaste for nonconformity although her personal circumstances and a genuine sense of adventure enable her to evolve a less constricting view of acceptable behavior. The conflict between her growing independence and the values of her childhood continues throughout her career and explains, in part, the constant rhythm of progression and regression in her writing.

The fact that many critics of the period discourage her attempts to strike out in new directions at the same time that they praise the less innovative aspects of her work clearly contributes to her persistent vacillation.[1] All writers are sensitive to the opinion of the critic—even when they proclaim their indifference—but in Espina's case, the lack of contact with other writers who share the same general philosophy of art, in combination with an awareness of her own deficient preparation, make her particularly susceptible to the influence exerted by critical literature. Her letters to Eduardo Gómez de Enterría demonstrate clearly the extent to which she is concerned with the views of her critics.[2] Although she continues to experiment with new forms, themes, and styles, it is always with a moderation that inhibits full exploration of her artistic possibilities. Her best works are precisely those in which she abandons the pattern established in her early production but all too often, she fails to sustain fruitful directions once initiated. Frequently, Espina regresses to a more conventional treatment within a single novel, creating a disconcerting and unacceptable fusion of two disparate modes. At other times, she follows her initial impulse throughout the novel but abruptly reverts to more traditional artistic orthodoxy in her subsequent publication. The repetitiousness that many critics have observed in her production is there, but accompanied by a persistent search for new approaches. This second aspect of her work, though artistically significant, has been generally ignored in the critical literature.

Among the many conventional, sometimes mediocre, pages in Concha Espina's works, she has left at least one outstanding novel and a number of very solid pieces. Artistically, she represents the link that joins nineteenth- and twentieth-century Spanish literature and also the introduction of the middle-class Spanish woman into the literary world. Emilia Pardo Bazán is in many respects of greater stature as an artist, but as an aristocrat, she was not subjected to many of the constraints that Concha Espina was forced to combat. Although Concha Espina is only partially successful in overcoming the limitations of her particular circumstances, her failures are ultimately beneficial since they provide a negative model for younger generations of women writers. On the other hand, her successes stand out as solid evidence of a talent that might have been more fully realized but which nonetheless on a number of occasions brought forth works of lasting value.

Notes and References

Chronology

1. There is an amazing discrepancy among critics with respect to the dates of principal events in Concha Espina's life. Unfortunately, Josefina de la Maza makes almost no mention of specific dates in her biography. For the most part, I have been able to reconstruct the chronology, but for the period between 1895 and 1904, the lack of accurate information forces me to give two possible years for the events.

Chapter One

1. Unless otherwise indicated, the information for Concha Espina's biography comes from Josefina de la Maza, *Vida de mi madre, Concha Espina* (Madrid, 1969).
2. These letters have been recently published by Alicia Canales, *Concha Espina* (Madrid, 1974), pp. 157-75.
3. Concha Espina, "Algunas noticias de mi vida y de mi obra," *Lecturas* (March, 1928), 321.
4. Concha Espina, *Lecturas*, 326.
5. de la Maza, p. 72.
6. Gerardo Diego, *"Prólogo"* in *Centenario de Concha Espina: Edición y antología* (Santander, 1970), p. xiii.
7. See his prologue to Concha Espina's *Obras completas* (Madrid, 1970), p. x. Hereafter, the volume and page number for all references to Concha Espina's *Obras completas* [*Complete works*] will be indicated in the text.
8. Concha Espina, *Lecturas*, 326.

Chapter Two

1. See "A la virgen de mi altar" ["To the virgin of my altar"] or "A la virgen dolorosa" ["To the suffering virgin"] in *Mis flores* (Valladolid, 1904).
2. See "Mis anhelos" ["My desires"]. Here, as elsewhere, the translations to English are my own.
3. I use the term Romantic here to include both the early Romantics and the postRomantic poets Bécquer and Rosalía de Castro.
4. Diego, p. xi.
5. See his prologue to Alicia Canales' book, p. 15.

6. Eugenio de Nora, *La novela española contemporánea,* I (Madrid, 1963), p. 331.

7. Nora, p. 331.

8. A. H. Clarke, "Naturaleza y paisaje: Un aspecto desatendido del arte descriptivo de las primeras novelas de Concha Espina," *Boletín de la Biblioteca de Menéndez Pelayo,* XLV (1969), 39.

9. See S. L. Millard Rosenberg, "Concha Espina, Poet Novelist of the *Montaña,*" *The Modern Language Forum* (April, 1922), p. 77. Also Father Félix García, "De 're' literaria," *España y América* (1926), p. 355.

10. Father Graciano Martínez, *De paso por las bellas artes,* II (Madrid, n.d.), pp. 291-95.

Chapter Three

1. It is doubtful that Concha Espina had more than a superficial knowledge of these philosophers. Her repudiation of their vision of life appears to be based more on generalized knowledge than on a firsthand acquaintance with their work.

2. Rosenberg, p. 77.

3. Concha Espina's definition of the term "feminine" does not coincide with the meaning given to it by the critics who employ it in discussing her novels. It reflects her desire to disassociate herself from the feminist movement while agreeing in principle with many of its concepts.

4. See José Alemany, "Voces de Maragatería y de otra procedencia usadas en *La esfinge Maragata,*" *Boletín de la Real Academia Española,* II (1915), 627-45.

5. *Vos* is the now obsolete form of address previously used when speaking to individuals of higher social rank.

6. See Rosenberg, p. 78. Also Rafael Cansinos Assens, *Literaturas del Norte: La obra de Concha Espina* (Madrid, 1924), p. 108.

7. In *Concha Espina. De su vida. De su obra al través de la crítica universal* (Madrid, 1928), p. 106.

8. This view is expressed by Ricardo León in *Concha Espina. De su vida,* p. 110.

9. Consuelo Berges, *Escalas* (Buenos Aires, 1936), p. 176.

10. See Charles Wesley Smith, *Concha Espina and Her Women Characters* (Ph.D. dissertation, George Peabody College for Teachers, Nashville, Tennessee, 1923), p. 80.

11. Diego, p. xxvi.

12. As already indicated, this trait also appears in *The Woman and the Sea.*

13. See Cansinos Assens, pp. 114-15. Also Ernest Boyd, *Studies from Ten Literatures* (New York, 1925), p. 134.

14. Rosenberg, p. 77.

15. Diego, p. xxvii.

16. Concha Espina, *Lecturas*, 327.
17. L. A. Warren, *Modern Spanish Literature*, I (London, 1929), 304.

Chapter Four

1. The term *jayón* is a regional word used to indicate children who were abandoned on the doorstep of a local home with the hope that the inhabitants would adopt the child as their own.
2. Diego, p. xxxi.
3. Cansinos Assens, p. 124.
4. Smith, p. 17.
5. Cansinos Assens, p. 124.
6. I use natural as in harmonious, "as it should be," not to imply a biological determinism as in naturalism.
7. Diego, p. xxii.
8. Nora, p. 335.
9. See Smith, p. 9.
10. Concha Espina, *Lecturas*, p. 323.
11. Helen S. Nicholson, "The Novel of Protest and the Spanish Republic," *University of Arizona Bulletin* (July 7, 1939), p. 13.
12. Nora, p. 336.
13. Although a number of critics praise Espina's use of a highly specialized vocabulary, Graciano Martínez (p. 338) is not alone in his criticism of what he refers to as "cheap knowledge extracted from an encyclopedia." Once more, the novelist's efforts to widen the scope of her work—in this case an extremely successful effort—meet with the prejudice of those who would deny women access to this type of knowledge.

Chapter Five

1. de la Maza, p. 72.
2. See Graciano Martínez, Rosenberg, and Félix García among others.
3. This story is not included in *Obras completas* but appears in the original version of *Pastorelas* (Madrid, 1920), p. 309.
4. Rosenberg, p. 80.
5. Cansinos Assens, p. 136.
6. Rosenberg, p. 80.
7. See Diego, p. xxxiv. Also Joaquín de Entrambasaguas y Peña, *Las mejores novelas contemporáneas*, IV (Barcelona, 1959), 1127.
8. This story is not included in her *Obras completas* but appears in the original edition of *Simientes* (Madrid, 1922), pp. 80-86.
9. This story is also omitted from *Obras completas*. See *Simientes*, pp. 109-18.

10. Consuelo Berges, "El 'caso' de Concha Espina," *Insula* (15 de junio, 1955), p. 8.

11. Early is used here to distinguish the neoRomantic writers of the *folletín* from their predecessors: Espronceda, Larra, Bécquer, etc.

12. M. H. Abrams, "English Romanticism: The Spirit of the Age" in *Romanticism Reconsidered* (New York, Columbia University Press, 1963), pp. 56-57.

13. Diego, pp. xxxiv-xxxv.

14. Pedro Laín Entralgo, *La generación del noventa y ocho* (Madrid, Espasa-Calpe, 1967), pp. 172 ff.

Chapter Six

1. The *wandervogel* was an old German association founded to encourage love of nature and knowledge of the country. Each Spring hundreds of young students took to the roads with knapsacks and spent several weeks traveling the rural areas of Germany.

2. Diego, p. xxxv; Nora, pp. 339-40.

3. Smith, p. 65.

4. Félix García, *Primavera en Castilla* (Madrid, n.d.), p. 65.

5. See her comments on *The Prudent Virgin* and feminism in general in *Lumen* (September, 1929), pp. 39-42.

6. It should be noted that Concha Espina's attitude toward the military has changed greatly since her early poems.

7. Entrambasaguas, p. 1231.

8. Félix García, *Al través de almas y libros* (Barcelona, 1935), p. 117; Rosenberg, p. 81.

9. Diego, p. xxxv.

10. See *Lumen*, 39-42.

11. *Singladuras* (Madrid, 1932), pp. 198-99.

Chapter Seven

1. A *romance* is a poem in octosyllabic meter with alternate assonance. It is the traditional poem of popular poetry.

2. See her interview with James O. Swain. "A Visit to Concha Espina at Luzmela," *Hispania* (December, 1934), p. 337.

3. The quote comes from *Vida del Escudero Marcos de Obregón* by Vicente Espinel and serves as the inscription to the second part of *Retaguardia* (*OC*, I, 1024).

4. Concha Espina makes no distinction between Republican and Communist.

5. This novel is not included in her *Obras completas*. It was originally published in Burgos, 1938. The quotes are taken from a note added at the end of the novel, entitled *"Homenaje"* ["Homage"], p. 185.

Chapter Eight

1. Both works were originally published in Madrid, 1942.
2. *La otra* [The other one], p. 155.

Chapter Nine

1. Entrambasaguas, p. 1236.
2. Gerardo Diego, on p. xxxvi, observes a similarity between Concha Espina and Pereda in some of her earlier novels. I find it much stronger in *A Valley in the Sea*.
3. Diego, p. xxxviii.

Chapter Ten

1. I would like to clarify that Spanish critics were no guiltier in their sexist treatment of Concha Espina than some of their counterparts in other countries. For a sample of United States sexism in literary criticism, see Swain, pp. 335-40.
2. María Cruz García de Enterría, "Unas cartas de Concha Espina," *Boletín de la Biblioteca de Menéndez Pelayo*, XLIII (1968), 283-306.

Selected Bibliography

PRIMARY SOURCES

Obras completas. Madrid: Edicion FAX, 1972. Vol. I-II.
Mis flores. Valladolid: La libertad, 1904.
Pastorelas. Madrid: Gil Blas, 1920.
Simientes. Madrid: Renacimiento, 1922.
"Algunas noticias de mi vida y de mi obra," *Lecturas* (March, 1928), 321-28.
Lumen. (September, 1929). Entire issue dedicated to Concha Espina. Includes interviews and speeches given by the novelist during her tour of the Caribbean countries.
Copa de horizontes. Madrid: Iberoamericana, 1930.
Singladuras. Madrid: Iberoamericana, 1932.
Esclavitud y libertad—Diario de una prisionera. Valladolid: Reconquista, 1938.
Alas invencibles. Madrid: Afrodisio Aguado, 1938.
Moneda blanca y La otra. Madrid: Afrodisio Aguado, 1942.

SECONDARY SOURCES

BERGES, CONSUELO. "El 'caso' de Concha Espina." *Insula* (July, 1955), pp. 1 and 8.
——— *Escalas*. Buenos Aires: Talleres Gráficas, 1930. As Concha Espina's secretary during the final years of the novelist's career, Berges gives some interesting insights into her work habits as well as some penetrating remarks on the quality of her work.
BOYD, ERNEST. *Studies from Ten Literatures*. New York: Scribners, 1925. One of the few studies published in English of any merit. Marred by faulty reading of several novels and limited in its coverage.
BOUSSAGOL, G. "Mme. Concha Espina." *Bulletin Hispanique* 25 (1913), 149-67. Brief but good discussion of Concha Espina's works up to and including *Mariflor*.
CANALES, ALICIA. *Concha Espina*. Madrid: E.P.E.S.A., 1974, Repeats much of the biographical information already contained in Josefina de la Maza's study but offers previously unpublished letters and a good introductory study by José Gerardo Manrique de Lara.
CANSINOS ASSENS, RAFAEL. *Literaturas del norte: La obra de Concha Espina*. Madrid: Crisol, 1924. The most complete study of her novels.

Limited in value due to excessive stress on the "Northern" character of her writing.

Concha Espina. De su vida. De su obra al través de la crítica universal. Madrid: Renacimiento, 1928. Contains excerpts from books and articles on the author. Compiled by her publisher and naturally biased. Useful in the biographical section and as a compendium of critical opinion.

DIEGO, GERARDO. *Centenario de Concha Espina: Edición y antología.* Santander, 1970.

—— "Homenaje a Concha Espina." *Boletín de la Biblioteca de Menéndez Pelayo* XLV (1969), 15-33.

—— "Poesía y novela de Concha Espina." *Insula* (July, 1955), pp. 1 and 8. All of Gerardo Diego's studies stress lyrical over narrative aspects of Concha Espina's work. Often accurate in his comments on style but rarely in his evaluation of a novel's merit.

ENTRAMBASAGUAS Y PEÑA, Joaquín de, ed. *Las mejores novelas contemporáneas.* Barcelona: Planeta, 1959. vol. IV. Most complete and best study on Concha Espina's work although often excessively uncritical.

ENTERRÍA, MARÍA CRUZ GARCÍA DE. "Unas cartas de Concha Espina." *Boletín de la Biblioteca de Menéndez Pelayo* XLII (1967), 283-306. Letters to a literary critic that are of value in reconstructing the novelist's ideas on the narrative.

GARCÍA, FÉLIX. *Al través de almas y libros.* Barcelona, 1925.

—— "Del 're' literaria." *España y América* IV (1926), 355-65.

—— "Examen de libros." *Religión y Cultura* IV (April, 1929), 115-19.

—— *Primavera en Castilla.* Madrid: Biblioteca Nueva, n.d. Exemplifies the sexist criticism that characterizes many studies of the novelist.

MAZA, JOSEFINA DE LA. *Vida de mi madre, Concha Espina.* Madrid: Magisterio Español, 1969. Only reasonably accurate account of the novelist's life. Extremely biased evaluation of her works and general significance.

MARTÍNEZ, GRACIANO. *De paso por las bellas artes.* vol. II Madrid: Imprenta del Asilo de Huérfanos, n.d. Exemplifies the traditional approach to literature written by a woman.

NORA, EUGENIO DE. *La novela española contemporánea.* vol. I Madrid: Gredos, 1963. Many errors in biographical data. Good analysis of Concha Espina's significance but limited to only a few novels.

ROSENBERG, S. L. MILLARD. "Concha Espina: Poet-Novelist of the *Montaña.*" *Modern Language Forum* (April, 1933), 76-81. The most complete study available in English. Many questionable affirmations and in general, excessively uncritical.

SMITH, CHARLES WESLEY. *Concha Espina and her Women Characters.* Ph.D. dissertation, George Peabody College for Teachers, 1933. Very weak study but well distributed to university libraries. Stresses excessively the moral implications of Concha Espina's novels, often based on an erroneous interpretation.

Index